"SPEAK EASY addresses the important elements of good communication both at work - and outside of the workplace as well. It provides a solid foundation of communication techniques and very specific examples of how to put them into practice. In simple, direct language, it helps the reader achieve a communication style and ability that translates into career- and life- success."

Melinda Wolfe, Senior Human Resources Executive, has held strategic roles in Diversity and Talent Development for GOLDMAN SACHS, AMERICAN EXPRESS and BLOOMBERG.

"This book is a communication tour de force. Cynthia Friedlander brings her years of coaching and communicating expertise to deliver a wide range of advice, tips, and best practices for professionals of every stripe. This is not a skim across the surface but a deep dive into all the ways that communication can be used and fine-tuned for professionals. From choosing the right words to being in the right state of mind, no topic is too small or too large for her to cover in depth. SPEAK EASY is a book that professionals and coaches will recommend and use for many years to come. Reserve a prominent place on your bookshelf for this instant business classic."

Mark Sirkin, Ph.D., international business coach and lecturer; author of dozens of professional articles and the book, THE SECRET LIFE OF CORPORATIONS: UNDERSTANDING THE TRUE NATURE OF BUSINESS; Director, Leadership and Organization Development practice for HILDEBRANDT INTERNATIONAL

"From beginning to end, Cindy hits on the key rules that everyone needs to know to be successful. Her summation that "Enhancing the way we communicate is the essential first step to self-development, interpersonal relationships, stress management, career navigation and simply getting through each day." is right on point!

For me, meeting Cindy and getting the knowledge that she shares so gracefully has opened up a whole new world that I had not dreamed could possibly be. Honing my communication skills truly has helped me tap into a new career as well as new friendships."

Bernice Smith, Director of Employee Services and Conflict Resolution, HARPO STUDIOS, HARPO INC.

"Cynthia Friedlander has given us all an enormous gift by writing SPEAK EASY. Often times, it is not a skill or experience gap that affects career advancement, it is the effectiveness of communication and relationship building that can either derail a career or propel an individual to success. Cindy has identified various communication styles (and their underlying causes) in an engaging manner and provides readers with practical techniques to improve the effectiveness of their communications. It is the lucky reader who benefits from the wisdom and insights that Cindy has gained through her years as a highly sought-after executive coach."

Cynthia Augustine, Senior Vice President, Human Resources and Employee Services, SCHOLASTIC Inc.; previously, SVP Talent Management, TIME WARNER, Inc. and SVP HR, THE NEW YORK TIMES

"Cynthia Leeds Friedlander is a communicator extraordinaire – I learn something each time Cindy and I talk – so when Cindy gave me her book to read, I had high expectations. There are many books on this topic as well as courses, seminars and speakers. I knew she wouldn't write a book on communication unless she had something to say. And she has said it as no one else can. SPEAK EASY has been a guide for me as well as a trusted tool."

Andrea Eisenberg, Career Management Consultant, EISENBERG RESOURCES / PREFERRED TRANSITION RESOURCES, former executive role with RIGHT MANAGEMENT

"Cynthia is a top-notch communicator! SPEAK EASY is packed with great stories and insights; it provides a quick how-to for improving your ability to communicate in professional and personal situations."

Christopher Williams, Director, Training and Development, Organizational Effectiveness, HOME BOX OFFICE - HBO

"The power of positive communication is far stronger when we can say, 'I agree with you.' as opposed to 'I do not disagree with you.' The lack of negativity fosters a safe haven for dialogue between people. I thank Cindy for pointing this out to me and helping me incorporate the power of positive dialogue in my communications with others. Her book, SPEAK EASY, encompasses so many aspects of communication and is such a valuable resource for everyone."

Mark Pedowitz, Senior Executive, ABC ENTERTAINMENT; former President ABC/TOUCHSTONE STUDIOS

SPEAK EASY

Cynthia Leeds Friedlander

The Communication Guide
for Career and
Life Success

The examples in this book are fictionalized and represent a wide range of situations and personalities. They are representative and stand for no specific actual individuals. The author cannot be held responsible for any interpretation or use of the book's content, suggestions and recommendations.

ISBN: 1-4392-3192-3
ISBN-13: 9781439231920

Visit www.wordcraftpress.com to order additional copies.

WORD
CRAFT
PRESS

For Daddy

I dedicate this book to my father who first showed me the two-way street of communication. Daddy often cited this Voltaire quote, "I may not agree with what you say but I will defend until death your right to say it." With my father, I could always voice my desires and passions without fear, no matter how different they were from his. He always listened and responded without judgment. Above all, there was respect.

Saying Thank You

Thank you, Robin, for rekindling the dream.

Thank you, Mother, for always believing.

Thank you, Neil, for being a word man.

Thank you, Jay, for saying it straight.

Thank you, Melinda, for providing the glue.

Thank you, Ronni, for the finishing touch.

Thank you, Megan, for partnering with patience.

Contents

Invitation To A Journey

When people ask me how long I've been a communication coach, I always answer, playfully, "Since I was three years old."

My sister was seven years older than I. She often antagonized people, especially our parents, by the way she communicated. She had endless curiosity which prompted many challenging questions and she wanted to have the last word in every conversation. "Why should I do that?", "Why are you doing that?", "Why can't I do that?", "Well, I think you're wrong!"

Instinctively, I set out to protect her from the aftermath of how she expressed herself, without any awareness of how young and inexperienced I was, "Don't say that." "You're going to make them angry." "Please just listen and don't talk back!"

Imagine the resentment that grew between us. Who wanted a three-year-old sister telling her what to say?

In looking back, even when quite young, I possessed two key ingredients for good communication that my sister lacked. The first was self-assurance. My family members tell me that, as a little girl, I used to greet them affectionately, saying, "You love me, donchya?" ("don't you?"). Coupled with my confidence, I had an intuitive sense of what others wanted and of what they were feeling or experiencing. I somehow knew what to say that would have the right impact on them, would be mutually pleasing, and would resonate authentically for me and for them. I've always had a keen awareness of the impact words have on people.

Daniel Goleman, a renowned psychologist and visiting instructor at Harvard, identified that awareness of others as a critical component of Emotional Intelligence, the primary subject of his extensive writing.

Many years have passed since those days of the three-year-old coach. I've spent my life honing the skills that came naturally to me as a child. My roles in life have been varied: friend, family member, student, team member, leader, salesperson, actress, wife, teacher, mother, graduate student, counselor, writer, coworker, employer, public speaker, seminar facilitator, trainer, career advisor, executive coach, management consultant. The umbrella of communication has always been the controlling influence over every aspect of my life.

Communication

Clients often say, "You've captured exactly what I want to say; the words roll off your tongue so easily. Couldn't you just go say those words for me? I'll never be able to say that as easily and well as you just did." I always laugh, supportively and appreciatively, and answer that of course the words come easily for me, that I've spent years focusing on better ways to communicate, and that I'm acutely attuned to all the layers that go into communication. As I continue to encourage them and review new ways to communicate with them, I watch as they take ownership of the words they actually want to say, conveying what they truly wish to express. I see the lights shining in their eyes and I see the

whoever edited this book should quit their job...

genuineness and strength they gain as they enhance their communication and get in touch with all of the elements that contribute to how they're expressing themselves and how they're being perceived.

> *Bella, a Marketing Director who had abruptly and unexpectedly lost her senior position in a technology company at age forty-five, described to me the value she'd gained from learning how to reposition what she wanted to convey to people. She described how much easier it had become for her to initiate difficult communications and how differently she felt about herself as a result of these enhanced techniques:*

> *"It's not whether my mood is up or down, it's the fact that my choice of language or vocabulary greatly influences how the person I'm speaking to perceives me, hears my message, and understands the events I am describing. It's about selecting appropriate language for that forward-moving spirit that I want to convey. This is not to ignore the fact that there's something that is painful or difficult, but to have a set of language to use for the outside world that works for me. It's how we all survive!"*

My work has enriched my life profoundly and now it's time to give back for all that I've gained. My gift of a lifetime's

What a bland world it would be if everyone was stripped of their unique quirks and molded into cookie-cutter personalities

work and dedication is **Speak Easy - The Communication Guide for Career and Life Success.** My goal is that you will find, understand, and be able to use all that you seek from this book so that you can easily say what you want and say it well, and mean what you say and say it directly.

And so, I'm inviting you to come on a journey with me. We will start our voyage with **The Basics**, the core mechanisms of effective communication. We will identify the four main underpinnings for every good communication. We will look at the most troublesome habits that deter successful communication and how to change them. We will pull together the key elements to provide you with a solid structural foundation for all of your communications.

Secondly, we will go to **The Human Side** of communication, to the interplay between our emotional make-up and our internal dialogues, and their effect on how and what we communicate. We will see the communication benefits gained from new perspectives and from defining, appreciating and leveraging our unique styles.

Lastly on this journey, we will look at **The Situations** where enhanced communication will set us apart and bring tremendous benefit. In my work as a Career Advisor and Communication Coach, I've primarily focused on work environments and work situations. Consequently, it's a natural outcome that the situations in this third section of **Speak Easy** will demonstrate a heavy emphasis on work-related circumstances and illustrations.

Certainly the five selected situations will bring you great benefit as critical competencies for good career management and significant platforms for exceptional communication:

- Refusing appropriately
- Networking effectively
- Workplace professionalism
- Negotiating/reaching agreement
- Public speaking/presentation

I've chosen these specific categories because of the

- ✓ Relevance of good communication to success in each of them
- ✓ Solid experience and expertise I can bring to you concerning them
- ✓ Frequency that people want help to master them

What I've always seen is that the person each of us is at work and the one we are outside of work is a single individual with similar communication characteristics and tendencies in both professional and non-professional environments. Consequently, it's extremely important to keep this book geared toward helping you become a better communicator in every aspect of your life.

Here are the critical **Speak Easy** objectives:

- To ensure the communication focus is solid, clear and consistent
- To speak to a wide audience with diverse roles and varied lifestyles
- To use the world of work as the primary framework for examining good communication

Additionally and significantly, **Speak Easy** is built on the *tried and true*. It encompasses much that has been laid out in varying communication, assertiveness, career, leadership, self-help, and business guides.

✓ What makes it innovative and original is its new presentation and distinct combination of information.
✓ What makes it accessible is its clear-cut simplification and creative illustration in friendly, straightforward and lasting ways.
✓ What makes it valuable is how it goes beyond what has previously been written to provide you with sharp insights and awareness for authentic, advantageous and comfortable communication.
✓ What makes it engaging and appealing is how it brings together the emotional and the practical so you can acquire new communication skills and simultaneously understand the underlying feelings that significantly influence your communication.

Let's begin our communication voyage. Let's look at the words we say and the frame we each bring to our communication through our own experiences and perspectives. Let's listen to our inner voices that accompany our viewpoints and our interactions with others. Let's look at how we express ourselves at home, at play and at work. Let's examine the threads of communication that weave into all parts of our lives and how we can create the communication tapestry that represents us well and authentically in all settings. Come join me on this wonderful trip of self-awareness, self-expression, and enhanced communication.

Ultimately, it's how we interact, connect and communicate with each other on this planet that will control our destiny. This is true from the smallest plane of our individual lives to the largest world platform. When those who do battle with each other, individually or on a grand scale, can sit down together and talk it out, the earth will be a better place.

Speak Easy:
The Basics

1 | Keep It Level

Sam is Director of Educational Services for a medium-sized nonprofit institution where pay is low and competition for recognition is high. Sam is a highly dedicated professional and takes his job seriously. His wife is a copywriter in an ad agency and they're expecting their second child. Sam feels a lot of pressure on the job and knows that his wife would like to be able to take a leave of absence to work part-time from home. She wants to be able to spend more time with the children for a few years. She feels like she can only do that if Sam is able to get a promotion at work or change jobs to make more money.

Sam has achieved significantly more credentials and experience than most of his superiors. Sam reports to Dena who is eight years younger than Sam. She has recently given Sam an extremely poor performance review and asked the Executive Director of the institution to be present for the review. Although Sam has exceeded the requirements for all of the deliverables for his job, his overall ratings are extremely low.

What Dena explains to Sam is that he's not seen as a team player and that his communication is viewed as unprofessional and uncooperative. He's told that people experience him as aloof and rigid and that his superiors think he's disrespectful of their authority and position. Sam decides to seek the help of a career coach so he can find a new job where his professionalism and expertise will be highly appreciated.

During the coaching process, Sam becomes more reflective and begins to think more carefully about the feedback in his review. He comes to the conclusion that he's had it with changing jobs to resolve difficulty; this isn't the first crossroads of this nature for Sam. He decides that the timing is right for him to look at how he contributes to the comments he's received in his performance review. Sam has heard these kinds of observations many times in the past. Sam knows he's been passed over often for promotions and realizes that although he's more professional, dedicated and qualified than others, there must be additional factors for why he isn't being promoted and why he continues to hear these types of descriptions about himself.

it all seems so clinical, impersonal, soulless, devoid of humanity

After a few sessions with his coach and after finding good ways to initiate open feedback conversations with current and former co-workers, Sam realizes that his communication is the main contributor to his obstacles at work. Even with his legitimate and accurate view of how less qualified, dedicated and smart many other people are in his work environment, Sam realizes that he's his own severest enemy in ways that are extremely counter productive.

Sam begins to understand that he's always been judgmental and has looked down on people younger and less experienced than he is. He's always worked extremely hard to achieve high grades in academic settings and sees that he's actually resentful of people who he thinks gain high marks or recognition with little effort.

Sam is always extremely well prepared for every contingency and often pushes ahead as if his way is the only way. His frequent base of operations is that others haven't thought the circumstances out as well as he has or are incapable of coming up with good solutions.

Sam also thinks that because his standards are so high that he must condemn or speak out, with what he comes to realize is disdain, if people are embracing standards that he considers lower than his own. He feels like no one will know what his views and standards are or that, even worse, people will think he's lowering his own standards, if he doesn't express his opposing views. Often it's only a look of contempt that he feels he must show in order to demonstrate how important it is to distance himself from what someone else has said or done.

As a result of these fiercely held principles, Sam realizes he almost always speaks down to others. He comes to realize how he's viewed as aloof. He recognizes that if he continues to communicate this way, few people will ever appreciate his expertise, his contributions, his work ethic or his professional values.

It takes time for Sam to achieve another way of interacting with people and it takes even longer <u>for others to accept the changes as authentic and reflective of who Sam really is.</u> Sam learns that it's better for him to work on solutions in his current environment with all of its challenges and

but is he correct? perhaps he needs to find a career where his exacting standards are a strength! not a perceived weakness (engineering) lol

reality check: once people have an impression of you, even if you change, their impression will never change, so you will have to move on elsewhere

realities. Within eighteen months, he earns a desired promotion and six months after that he accepts a new role in a new organization. Sam feels like he would never have gotten to these new places without chang-ing his basic way of communicating and without realizing the impact of his style on others.

The first fundamental element of good communication is:

> **1. No MATTER WHAT THE LEVEL OF POWER OR STATION IN LIFE OF THE OTHER PERSON IN A DIALOGUE, THE COMMUNICATION CAN ALWAYS BE LEVEL.**

Think of an equal sign with arrows pointing back and forth. See the equal, two-way street of communication in every type of conversation or verbal exchange.

Communication begins to break down when you feel an advantage over or disadvantage with another person. Either of these two imbalances may exist. Life is rarely fair or equal. People do have positions of authority or power.

Hierarchies abound: *fuck hierarchy, it is only a shared delusion*

♦Parent / Child ♦Teacher / Student ♦Employer / Employee
♦Owner / Buyer ♦Captain / Soldier ♦Senior / Freshman
♦President / Clerk ♦Boss / Secretary ♦Interviewer / Job Candidate ♦Expert / Lay Person ♦Celebrity / Unknown Individual ....and so on.

When people are on the offensive or the defensive, communications will weaken. When you see communication as an equal two-way back-and-forth exchange, both to listen and to be heard, respectfully, no matter what the circumstances, you will be able to say what you want appropriately and effectively. Good communication is never at the expense of self or others. *sure, Bill is great @ using his communication skills to sexually exploit women w/less power*

NOBODY DOES IT BETTER THAN BILL

One of the most well-known models of level communication is Bill Clinton. Forgetting political preferences and withholding judgment of character or choices, we can see a style of communication in Clinton that exemplifies the equal two-way street of communication. Whether talking to heads-of-state, the person in the street, or even to a child, Bill Clinton is known for communicating on an equal plane with people.

Ummm chars choices color everything

In his first televised Presidential debate, Clinton walked in front of his podium and spoke into the camera like he was in the voters' living rooms, having a conversation with them.

George Bush Senior, then President, spoke down from his podium with authority, resting in his position of power, without engaging the voter on a human level.

H. Ross Perrot lectured the voters from behind his podium, shaking a forefinger at them like a scolding parent to a misbehaving child.

MORE THAN WORDS

To achieve level communication, choosing the right words is extremely important. What is surprising, however, is that words are actually the smallest contributor to how communication is received. So how does this seeming contradiction work?

When people are asked to say what percentage of communication they think is non-verbal, what percentage is other than the spoken words, they usually recognize that the percentage has to be at least 50%. They frequently think it may even be in the 75% range. They're usually astounded to learn how much larger a portion it actually is.

I wonder how much this has changed in the age of digital communications? is there more recent data? ← 9 →

The second fundamental element of good communication, that research repeatedly shows, is:

> **2. THE NON-VERBAL PORTION OF COMMUNICATION EXCEEDS 90% OF HOW COMMUNICATION IS RECEIVED.**

The largest non-verbal elements of communication are <u>facial expression</u> and <u>tone of voice</u>.

As a dedicated wordsmith and communication coach, I remember first learning this percentage and feeling rather down-hearted. I said to a colleague, "What's the point in my helping people fine-tune the words they're using if the words represent only 7% of how communication is received?" My colleague quickly pointed out that if there's only a 7% window to get the right words into a communication, it's critical to choose those words carefully. His response crystallized for me the significance of choosing the right words, while always remembering the critical importance of tone and facial expression.

How Communication Is Received:

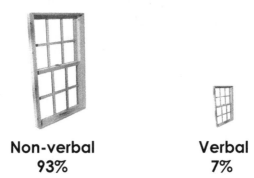

| **Non-verbal** | **Verbal** |
| 93% | 7% |

To gain a sense of confidence about how to achieve optimum communication that encompasses all of these

for someone who pushes that presentation is even more important than content, the author **★REALLY★** *should have picked a better font & layout for this book*

Cynthia Leeds Friedlander

nuances, always remember to **combine** the image of the **level two-way street** - to lay the foundation for the right words - with an awareness of the importance of the **non-verbal** elements of communication, especially the **tone** and **facial expression.** This correlates with our first and second fundamental keys to good communication from pages 7 and 10.

> **1. N**O MATTER WHAT THE LEVEL OF POWER OR STATION IN LIFE OF THE OTHER PERSON IN A DIALOGUE, THE COMMUNICATION CAN ALWAYS BE LEVEL.

> **2. T**HE NON-VERBAL PORTION OF COMMUNICATION EXCEEDS **90%** OF HOW COMMUNICATION IS RECEIVED.

ARROGANCE IS LETHAL
Confidence attracts. Arrogance repels. Where does one end and the other begin? People often resist using strong direct communication because they fear they will offend others or appear arrogant. They've been taught that modesty is a virtue and that it's wrong to "toot your own horn". Actually, arrogance almost never stems from confidence; rather, it usually indicates some type of insecurity. When people are truly confident in what they're expressing, there's no place for arrogance. When you believe whole heartedly in what you're saying, the resulting confidence is magnetic. Arrogance immediately distances others from you. Seeing yourself on a level playing field contributes to eliminating arrogance and engendering confidence. Compare these two statements, describing the same situation.

this is also very gendered

✗ "Did you know that I am the only one in my office who could figure out how to fix the printer? Nobody else had a clue what to do. It sure was good that I was there to save the day and save the company a lot of money too!"

✓ "I really enjoyed figuring out what was wrong with the printer. We all were baffled when it still didn't work after checking the ink cartridges, looking for a paper jam, and making sure the electrical connection was okay. I'm glad I got to use my detective, technical and engineering skills so we didn't have to pay outside sources to service the printer and to print our report. I just love being the go-to, fix-it person among all my coworkers."

GETTING RID OF THE SHOULDER CHIP

When people are wronged in some legitimate way and think that the principles they believe in passionately have been diminished by the communications of others, they often develop a chip on their shoulders. As a result, they then communicate in a way that works against the very values they hold so dear. Whenever you're coming from a self-righteous place of "How dare you!" or a victimized place of "Why me?", you will tend to diminish the cause you believe in most. A chip on the shoulder leads to judgmental communication. If you're judging others, you can't speak from a level place with them. If you're speaking from an unequal position in tone and demeanor, your communication will be weakened, you won't be heard in the way you desire, and your message will most likely be disregarded or diminished. Compare these two quite different ways of conveying almost identical messages:

✗ "You never call me anymore. You know I had to give up my car. I don't have anyone to drive me anywhere. I'm sure you could find some time to call and see how I am and offer to take me shopping when you go to the grocery store. If you cared about me, you would take me along when you go."

✓ "I miss hearing from you and wanted to call to find out how you are. Since I don't have my car anymore, I wanted to let you know how much I'd enjoy doing errands and shopping with you. If at any point that would work for you, it would be terrific. I know you travel for work and have such a demanding schedule. Sure would love to see you."

SUBSERVIENCE IS FOR PUPPY DOGS

distinction between servant leadership & subservience

Margaret is the Senior Vice President of Strategic Planning for an international financial services firm. She's loved by everyone in her firm and always looks for ways to make people's lives easier and better.

Margaret frequently works longer hours than her colleagues and the people who work for her. She rarely takes all of the vacation she's entitled to annually. She's sick several times a year which frequently results in her coming in to work prior to being well again. This is often followed by a longer period of a more severe illness, causing her to be away from work for an extended timeframe. She always works from home if she can't come in to the office. Her work never suffers because of these illnesses. She doesn't delegate anything because she feels that no one is as reliable as she is and she doesn't want to burden others.

Margaret is seen as indispensable. She's known for never saying no to anyone's requests no matter how high or low their position in the organization or in which department they work. She solicits input from others without asserting her views. She asks permission rather than states her goals and desires. She apologizes frequently without having committed offenses.

Everyone adores her sense of humor and good nature. Margaret is the kind of person who will give you her only pen if you don't have one with you and who will hand you a paper towel to dry your hands if she's standing at the next sink to yours when you're washing your hands.

Because of her dedication, loyalty, friendliness and availability to all, it's difficult to criticize Margaret. Yet, for some reason, Margaret is ill at ease in her workplace. She sees that others often take advantage of her and frequently her super heroic efforts aren't even appreciated. She feels that she lacks an executive presence. Even though she's quite happy in her current role and seeks no higher position, she'd still liked to be respected and appreciated on a different level than she senses currently exists. She'd also like to remain as dedicated without feeling frequently so exhausted, and at times being burnt-out.

What's going on here is simple. Margaret sees herself below others. She always puts her views second even when hers is the voice of authority. Her wonderful qualities that are admired and respected become warped by the fact that she never sees herself as equal or entitled. She's always trying to gain approval rather than focus on contributing her expertise. She's reticent to take credit. She wants to please at the expense of her health, professionalism and work priorities. The most astonishing and positive element of all of this is that Margaret is highly confident and passionate about both her work and her level of expertise. She knows how smart she is and knows how much she has to contribute. She provides us with an excellent representative *example of the negative results of subservient communication.*

Margaret wants to make changes in how she communicates and how she is being perceived, without giving up her level of dedication to her job and without diminishing her most important goal. Margaret likes to help others most of all.

The first objective is for Margaret to become self-aware, to see that her communication often has the opposite impact from the one she would most like. The second step is for Margaret to gain new ways to communicate in an equal two-way manner that feels authentic to her, to who she is, and to the values she holds dear.

✗ Instead of saying in an unsure tone and self-demeaning manner,

"I don't know if you might want to try this or not."

✓ Margaret can say with confidence,

"Here's what I see as a good solution to this situation."

✗ Instead of approaching a person who reports directly to her, in a childlike, supplicating way,

"I'm so sorry and feel I have to apologize to you for the technology department who did not run our numbers and complete our report for us. I hope you aren't upset by my asking you to do this work manually and get the report ready for our meeting

> *tomorrow morning. I'm so sorry that I have to ask you at the last minute. I feel so bad about your being loaded up with extra work today."*

✓ Margaret can make the same request to this person who works for her, in a level, authoritative, mutually respectful tone:

> *"Since technology didn't run our numbers for us, I'm asking you to complete the report we need for tomorrow's meeting manually. This was totally unexpected, so it's absolutely fine for you to shift your other priorities to make this happen. I appreciate whatever juggling is required to get this done and want you to know that I recognize the need for that. Let me know if this change in your day affects other people and I'll speak to them about what I've requested you to do today. Again, thank you very much for doing this."*

Subtle differences in tone and words can make a big difference in how we feel about ourselves and our work and most of all in the way people perceive us.

What is it that makes us love dogs? Certainly we adore the unconditional adoration our dogs give us. Those shiny eyes that look up into our faces as if to tell us, "I'll do anything you want no matter what you say or do to me."

As endearing as it is for a dog to be constantly ready to do our bidding and please us, such a cloying servitude in human beings can have a quite negative effect. Just as arrogance is repellent, subservience can be equally distasteful. Expressing yourself in a lowly, apologetic, victimized or lesser style will turn your communication into unnecessary and unappreciated begging, pleading, apologizing or explaining. Communicating in an equal and level tone will demonstrate self-respect and respect for the other person, and will generate the highest potential for getting that respect returned. Using level two-way communication in its most optimum manner always includes being polite and demonstrating total respect for yourself and others.

THE GOAL ON EACH SIDE OF THE EQUATION
The equal two-way symbol can be a constant reminder that in every dialogue, there are two sides.

The more you recognize what the other person wants and can communicate that you've actually heard what that is, the more legitimacy you give to your own position, no matter how it may differ from the other person's view.

One of the most frequent instances of unbalanced communication is the job interview. For some reason, people tend to feel that they're in such a lesser and disadvantaged position when they're on job interviews. They completely forget the main aspect of what they're doing which is having a conversation.

Here's how the two-way symbol representing a job interview works:

INTERVIEWER: Looking for the right employee for the job.
INTERVIEWEE: Looking for the right employer & the right job.

By looking at the job interview in this equal way from both perspectives, it's easy to embrace the concept of two-way and level communication. Is there a differentiation of power in the job interview? Of course there is. As the interviewee, you don't have the power to make them give you the job. And the interviewer does have the power to give the job to you or to someone else. It's the communication in the job interview that can be completely equal. It's up to you to open up this view of communication to yourself and use it to your benefit in all types of situations.

In every shared dialogue, there are two sides and it's through effective communication that each of those sides can gain legitimacy and equality no matter what the actual content or eventual outcome.

Speak Easy Rules

Review and Summary:

1 | Keep It Level

✓ Experience a level playing field of communication.

✓ Be aware of how facial expressions say more than words.

✓ Monitor your voice tone to diminish dual messages.

✓ Express your reactions directly without apology.

✓ Focus on demonstrating respect in every communication.

2-way communication is very difficult when the other person speaks in monosyllables & obviously not engaged

— what are strategies for engaging a noncommittal conversational partner?

this entire vignette is fucking toxic
the person that needs an attitude
adjustment is STEVE not Terry

2 | Tell Them That You Really Heard

this dynamic sounds like an abusive relationship

Terry is the Creative Director for a textile manufacturer. He's worked for the company for sixteen years. He has a rare combination of superlative management skills and exceptional creative vision. He's seen as a stable force and a calming presence by his department and by others outside of his department as well. In contrast, there's always a good deal of frenzy and static among the upper ranks of the company.

Recently a management consulting firm was brought in to revitalize the business and make recommendations on how the executive team could be more effective. The current management structure has mandated a closer working relationship between Terry and Steve, the Director of Marketing. Many people describe Steve as a manager who often communicates disrespectfully and who leads dictatorially.

Steve often blurs the lines between Marketing and Creative and makes broad pronouncements about visuals and print production that are out of *his area of jurisdiction and way out of his area of expertise. He mainly does this to position his authority. Basically, he likes being the commandant.*

In a planning meeting that includes Steve, Terry, and the company President, Sarah, Terry presents the mockup for the spring catalog. Suddenly, in the middle of Terry's presentation, in front of all the senior executives in the room, Steve slams his fist on the table and screams out attackingly, "How many times do I have to say this?! I don't ever want to see a single photo fill a full page in any of our catalogs and I never want to see a line of print across any of our products!"

Terry's face begins to flush. He's sick of Steve making blanket proclamations publicly about creative decision-making for the company catalog. Terry decides to refrain from yelling back at Steve and to state facts as calmly and as simply as he can. He knows there's anger in his voice when he answers, "Steve, there are definitely going to be times when a full-page photo is exactly the right visual choice and there are many ways to place print across a product that are elegant, strong, appropriate and optimum. This just isn't your decision to make!"

Steve backs down and calms down, accompanied by a good amount of what appears to be sulking and resentment. Terry can feel that his blood pressure has risen significantly. He wants to handle these conversations differently to protect his health and to protect his job. He definitely wants to stop sounding angry when he speaks to Steve. He knows that Sarah and Steve see eye-to-eye on almost everything. Everyone knows that Sarah views Steve as her right hand guy and as the number two person in the company. Terry often sees Sarah fold her arms across her chest and scowl in these meetings whenever he goes toe-to-toe with Steve.

He decides that he would benefit tremendously from outside professional support to help him gain perspective. He wants to learn how to assert his Creative leadership. Terry also knows how important it is that others, particularly Sarah, view him as a collaborator.

Partnering with an executive coach, Terry realizes that even though asserting his position and authority is his primary goal, he will gain the most if he can show that he's listening to Steve by validating what Steve says. He recognizes that he can acknowledge what's important to Steve without

wait — why the fuck are we coddling and acquiescing to the guy w/anger issues who is creating a toxic work environment??

fuck that

agreeing with him or acquiescing to what Steve wants him to do. He can be appreciated for being collaborative, without giving up his authority and visual integrity.

The next time Steve explodes, Terry says, genuinely and without anger, "Steve, I hear how strong your views are about full page photos in the catalog and I know that you don't like it when we use them. I'm respectful of your opinion and know it's important for you to convey to me what your beliefs are. I'm certainly open to incorporating those beliefs when I can. Here are our visual goals for the catalogue: to set us apart from our competition, to make sure there's variety in our pages, and to create an overall look that matches our branding and our mission. This type of photography use and print layout accomplishes these important objectives.

As much as I always respect and welcome your input, it's my role to set the creative tone for the company. I want to keep these pages as designed and presented. My team and I have worked diligently for many hours to produce them."

Terry suddenly realizes how much he's accomplished by responding with this new approach. He's amazed by how calm he feels when he replies to Steve this way. Terry understands that to validate whatever Steve is saying requires actively listening to and concentrating on Steve's comments and reactions so that Terry's response can specifically reflect what Steve has said. Terry can feel that his blood pressure has remained relaxed and normal in spite of Steve's fist-slamming trademark which has always sent Terry's heartbeat racing in the past. As Terry is responding, he notices Sarah lean into the conference table, nod her head in approval and break into a big grin. Terry is calm, cool, and collected when he replies.

Terry's biggest take-away is the knowledge that he's the only person he can control. What's so amazing is that he also experiences how much positive influence he can have on Steve's abrasive communication style by simply remembering to validate Steve prior to stating what his own views are. And the best part of all is yet to come. Steve rarely, if ever, will pound his fist down again when he talks to Terry. In the future, even when Steve disagrees with an approach that Terry is taking, Steve will say what he has to say to Terry in a much more relaxed and respectful tone.

that sounds like pure fantasy

Terry's story brings us to the third fundamental element of good communication:

> **3. VALIDATING AND ACKNOWLEDGING WHAT THE OTHER PERSON THINKS OR WANTS IS OF EQUAL IMPORTANCE TO THE TWO-WAY STREET OF LEVEL COMMUNICATION.**

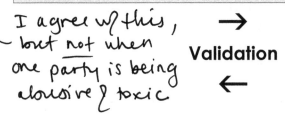

I agree w/ this, but not when one party is being abusive & toxic

→
Validation
←

When you're talking to someone, your views of the world may differ tremendously from that person's perspectives. Even our soul mates can have opposite viewpoints from our own. In most communications, we become so eager to have our say that we can only focus on what our own point of view is and we rush ahead without any validation of the other person in the dialogue.

So many communications repeatedly turn into nonproductive duels like the confrontation described between Terry and Steve. In these, the two-way street loses its level equality to look like this:

→ | ←

Or like this:

↘ | ↖

Or like this:

↗ | ↙

Experiencing the equal sign with its two-way arrows and re-membering to start your communication with a validation of the other person will dramatically improve all of your interactions and will significantly enhance the way you feel about yourself and how others see you.

Validation

What quickly becomes clear is that sincere and authentic validation and acknowledgement require giving focused attention to what the other person is expressing. And so, we have arrived at the fourth fundamental element of good communication:

> **4.** *THE BASIC KEY TO SUCCESSFUL VALIDATION IS LISTENING.*

SUCCESSFUL VALIDATION

 =

LISTENING

It's impossible to validate someone sincerely and specifi-cally without listening attentively to what that person is say-ing. You can't simply start your response with a throw-away standard comment like "Yeah, I hear you." or "I understand what you're saying." You must show how well you've been listening and respond in a way that specifically and genu-inely shows that you've really heard.

Some good examples of VALIDATION statements are:

- ✓ "It's very clear how much you want to...
  (be specific)"
- ✓ "I can see how important it is to you to...
  (be specific)"
- ✓ "I know that your views about ...
  (be specific) are...(be specific)"
- ✓ "I recognize your perspectives about...
  (be specific) are ...(be specific)"
- ✓ "I certainly respect that you want to...
  (be specific)"

And no matter how differently you see the situation, it's critical to omit the word "but" as you make the transition from your validation to your viewpoint. "But" is a word that can negate whatever preceded it:

- ✗ "I know you want to go to the beach but I want to go to the mountains."
- ✓ "I know you want to go to the beach and I want to go to the mountains."

- ✗ "I know it's important to you to meet on Tuesdays but I prefer Thursdays."
- ✓ "I know it's important to you to meet on Tuesdays. I prefer Thursdays."

Eliminating one small word can change the dynamic from competitive and combative to a communication that is two-way and open. *that's overly simplistic*

MOVING THE SPOTLIGHT
Some people like to be the center of attention and others wish there were never a spotlight on them at all. If you can experience listening as if you're shining a spotlight on the

other person and then focus on describing what's in the spotlight, you will be able to validate people naturally. You will be concentrating on what the other person is saying and can then add strength to your own side of the situation by having first made the other person's position as meaningful as your own. Demonstrating mutual respect, refraining from being self-centered, and strengthening your own position by acknowledging other views are critical elements of **listening**.

a lot of these strategies require mutual trust & respect

be wary of black holes that suck up all light & never reflect it back (Trump)

THE ART OF REFLECTING BACK

When you show the other person that you're listening, you give that person the ability to listen to you without confrontation or defensiveness. By turning the spotlight away from yourself and on the other person, you also give your beliefs a platform to be acknowledged and appreciated reciprocally. When you mirror back to people what they've been saying to you, they feel heard and respected. The beauty of validation is that it reinforces the other person without requiring you to buy into a premise or provide solutions.

While these approaches are gender-free, there are stereotypes in styles of communication that may come to mind. Even with every good intention, these are actually counter to the art of validation and reflecting:

an opportunity, not a platform, which others may ignore

- There's the macho man who thinks he has to fix what's broken, provide a solution or lead the way.
  ✗ "What you should do to fix that is ..."

- There's the maternal woman who has to nurture or protect.
  ✗ "Oh poor you! I know exactly how that feels ..."

- There are those who insist on advising, judging or admonishing.
  ✗ "That would be a big mistake because ..."

The more you can listen and communicate what you've actually heard:

- The more options and perspectives you can offer others to consider
- The better a communicator you will become
- The less pressure you will experience about whether you are being a good communicator
- The more natural your communications will be
- The more receptive others will be to listen to what you have to say

ACKNOWLEDGEMENT DOESN'T MEAN AGREEMENT

Just because you validate what someone has said doesn't mean that you're in agreement with that position. Expressing acknowledgment for differing views generates receptivity from people with those views to listen to your ideas. No matter how high your standards and beliefs, your validation of differing viewpoints primarily demonstrates listening rather than signifies agreement.

it's a fine balance between acknowledgement & agreement, w/ different cultural, social, contexts

32

Saying It Without Judgment

It's intriguing to see that people frequently feel they're lowering their standards if they refrain from expressing judgment of behavior or attitudes that differ from their own. We saw just such a person in the opening illustration of Chapter One. Sam's communication was typical of those who think that if they aren't extremely harsh in their comments about a topic they care deeply about, no one will know how strong their feelings are about it. Most often, when individuals who've heard such judgmental criticism are asked their reactions, they report feeling a sense of being attacked rather than any respect for the person's beliefs or increased desire to follow that person's expressed goals. Intimidation and judgment reduce motivation.

Speak Easy Rules

Review and Summary:

2 | Tell Them That You Really Heard

✓ Acknowledge what others are saying.

✓ Validate others' positions before promoting your own.

✓ Concentrate on listening without jumping to your views.

✓ Realize you can validate others without agreeing with them.

✓ Separate high standards from disapproval and judgment.

these are generally good rules
of thumb, but tactics have to
shift depending on the psychological
profiles of those involved: trust/respect,
narcisicism, mob mentality, contrarianism,
brown-nosing, toxic viewpoints
(aka, I'm not going to "validate"
misogynstic/racist viewpoints)

THE FUNDAMENTALS REVISITED
(Chapter One)

1. NO MATTER WHAT THE LEVEL OF POWER OR STATION IN LIFE OF THE OTHER PERSON IN A DIALOGUE, THE COMMUNICATION CAN ALWAYS BE LEVEL.

2. THE NON-VERBAL PORTION OF COMMUNICATION EXCEEDS NINETY PERCENT OF HOW COMMUNICATION IS RECEIVED.

Non-verbal
93%

Verbal
7%

The Fundamentals Revisited

(Chapter Two)

---

3. *Validating and acknowledging what the other person thinks or wants is of equal importance to the two-way street of level communication.*

→

Validation

←

---

4. *The basic key to successful validation is listening.*

Successful Validation

 = Listening

3 | There's A Good Way
To Say Everything

Michelle is the Head of Programming for a nationally syndicated radio station based in Northern California. She also oversees the Traffic, Promotion and Community Affairs departments. Michelle has a strong work ethic and is dedicated to being the best professional she can be. She's proud of how well she selects talent. Indeed she has the best hiring record in the station in terms of turnover. It's rare for someone she's hired to leave his or her job or be lured away to a competing station.

Michelle interacts with others exactly the way she'd like to be treated by her managers and coworkers. She respects people's privacy and autonomy. She trusts they will do the right thing and that they will come to her if they have problems. One of her core beliefs is that if you hire the right people, and give them long leashes to do their jobs, the station will run itself. She's always calm under pressure and believes that everything happens for a reason and that *everything will eventually level out, given enough patience and time.*

She loves her job, although she often thinks about the old days when she was developing programming concepts and pitching ideas. She's sometimes baffled by how all of her time now is spent on tedious administrative detail and tiresome management accountability.

Her door is always open. The fact that people rarely come to see her in her office never crosses Michelle's mind as a concern. She has the "No news is good news"/"If it ain't broke, don't fix it." approach to work and to life.

She's the mother of two teenage children who describe her style of parenting almost exactly the way her coworkers and subordinates describe her style of management. Her children rarely bring their problems to their mother because they believe she will be disinterested in talking to them or helping them resolve their minor or major dilemmas.

Michelle openly says that she's conflict-avoidant. She will go 180 degrees in the opposite direction to avoid being part of, observing, or being asked to resolve any type of confrontation or disagreement. She believes that if you turn away from disputes, people will work things out for themselves. She almost never raises her voice or shows her emotions. She has few fluctuations in her even temperament.

When Michelle is one of four executives at the station selected for a 360-degree feedback program, she's quite pleased. She's eager to find out what she's doing well and how she can improve. When she sits down with her coach to review her 360-degree feedback report, she's rather shocked. It never occurred to her that all of the autonomy she'd given people was seen as disregard and lack of leadership. Michelle is stunned to learn that people see her as inaccessible and unavailable. Even though her door is always open, she sits at her computer facing away from the doorway and everyone thinks she's engrossed in what she's doing and doesn't want anyone to disturb her.

People say that they never bring problems to Michelle because they see her as someone who is uncommunicative and afraid to assert her-

self. They think she won't take needed action when there are problems that need resolving. They report that they never come to her with workplace issues or personal difficulties because they think she doesn't care and won't do anything to resolve the situation even if she did. What surprises Michelle the most about the feedback is that she learns that her boss thinks she's not on top of her job and that she's not keeping him informed at all.

Michelle embraces the coaching support that is provided to her following the 360-degree feedback. She asks the coach to help her be a better communicator and to tackle conflicts head on so she can change the perceptions people have about her. She realizes how valuable it is to initiate conversations and to ensure people she wants to participate in resolving problems. She sees how critical it is to convey what she's thinking and feeling so people will understand what her views are. She knows that if she communicates what's important to her and provides people with direction, resolution, decisiveness, and repercussions, she will earn the respect she'd always believed she had and that she merits.

It's eye-opening to Michelle to learn that without communication and action, her belief system and values will be unknown to others. She's most appreciative of these new insights when she realizes how applicable they are to her relationships with her children. It's hard for her to take in what her life would have been like if she'd never come to understand how beneficial it is to be an open and frequent communicator. She knows <u>that her natural style is to be a silent observer</u>. She now challenges her old belief that this was the way to empower others. She also knows that her fear of confrontation needs to be redefined and reinterpreted to prevent her from slipping back into her old comfort zones of avoidance and isolation. Michelle asks to be able to work with her coach for an extended timeframe so that she can turn her new awareness into consistent communication that's second nature for her. She knows it will take time, focus, dedication and determination.

then she should embrace that strength and surround herself w/ diverse & complementary styles to shore up her weak points, rather than reinventing herself into a cookie-cutter mold

If you carefully examine every challenging situation that you encounter, you will be able to find a way to express what you want to communicate about it in an appropriate and comfortable way. Usually, it's fear of confrontation coupled with distorted assumptions that create barriers to communication. These barriers subsequently lead to an erosion or escalation of the situation that currently exists, creating a self-sustaining downward spiral that can end up in a completely new place, dramatically different from the one that's optimum.

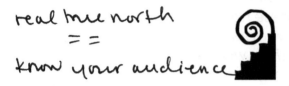

real true north
= =
know your audience

YOU CAN ALWAYS COUNT ON TRUE NORTH
(Southern charm definitely has its limitations)

The tendency to enhance or withhold the truth is a common occurrence which inevitably undermines optimum communication. In childhood, I was taught the importance of always telling the truth. In contrast, I was also taught the contradictory concept that telling a *white lie* is okay if it protects someone else's feelings or advances a certain benign type of self-protection. Growing up in southwestern Virginia, I often observed a style of Southern disingenuous charm that veiled the truth. "Y'all come see us, ya' hear? (pronounced 'hee-ah')" often actually meant, "We don't really want your type crossing our doorstep." Embellishing or distorting reality leads to trouble. Just like the children's story of Pinocchio whose nose would grow every time he told a lie, the effect of avoiding or obscuring the truth will take over and the stage will be set for distortion or misrepresentation. It will become increasingly difficult to remember what you've actually said and the truth will become dangerously elusive.

If the truth is your first constant, your goal can then be finding the right and best way to tell the truth. The promise of honesty is a significant one to make to yourself and to others. Never distort. Never misrepresent. Trust the compass of truth in all of your communications.

There are three key elements to remember to ensure the potential of having a direct communication:

good rules

1. Always start with the truth.
2. Define and identify what you most want to express.
3. Examine what you say to make sure it feels authentic and in sync with who you are.

If you look at the key elements of what you want to communicate and find neutral language that avoids irritation or aggravation, using a level tone of voice, you will find that telling the truth is easier and better than an elaborate fabrication you invent to make the communication seem more palatable for you and the other person. People will thank you and appreciate hearing the truth, directly, in the right way. Reminding yourself of the equal two-way street of communication and of the importance of validating the

LOL not all people

45

while I agree that direct honesty is often the best approach, there are a lot of cultural assumptions baked into this advice

other person remains the basic foundation for accomplishing the goal of truth in communication.

Validation

AVOIDANCE IS WORSE THAN CONFRONTATION

Avoiding communication or using indirect ways to express what you want to say will prolong the agony of a situation and usually be much worse than the actual conversation you're dreading so fiercely. How many times have you said to yourself, after finally having the courage to say something that you've been agonizing over and avoiding: "That wasn't as bad as I thought it would be!"? Or even better: "That was so much easier than I thought it would be and I feel so much better having gotten that off of my chest."? Facing reality and saying what you have to say directly almost always weighs less heavily than avoiding the encounter. Anticipation quite frequently weighs much more than actuality:

ACTUALITY

ANTICIPATION

TELLING TIME VERSUS MAKING THE WATCH

So often people answer a question or describe what's critical to them by continuing to describe and expand on what they've already said quite well. Sometimes this is caused by lack of confidence, feelings of guilt or discomfort in some way. They forget that "less is more." Obviously, either extreme – saying too little or too much – can be unappealing and unfruitful. Saying too little can be abrupt which can leave people hanging and thinking you're rude, rushed, curt or even superficial. Saying too much can dilute or sabotage what you want to say and can leave people annoyed, overwhelmed, or thinking you're boring, pedantic, overbearing, or even pushy.

The old admonition to KEEP IT SIMPLE is a good one. No one wants to be described as a person who tells you how to make a watch when asked what time it is.

 versus

ha! that's kind of good, but also, depends on the type of conversation

It's so critical to find the happy medium in communicating, to remain focused and to say just enough to crystallize exactly what you want to get across. The fairy tale of The Three Bears provides great reminders to avoid saying *too little* or *too much* and to focus on making sure you get your communication just right.

Speak Easy Rules

Review and Summary:

3 | There's A Good Way
To Say Everything

✓ Select direct ways to communicate.

✓ Realize that people appreciate hearing the truth.

✓ Recognize that there is no need to embellish or distort.

✓ Resolve to be comfortable talking about difficult topics.

✓ Use simpler descriptions and realize that less is more.

a lot of this advice is naive
& overly-simplistic, w/ little
acknowledgement of cultural
differences & nuances in communication
styles

true north is to actually always
know your audience

4 | Replace Damaging Habits

There are **10** basic tools in **The Speak Easy Toolbox** that can greatly enhance how you communicate. To acquire skill in using these tools, you may need at first to be quite self-conscious about each one and concentrate on incorporating each separately over time to gain a new natural repertoire. Since language patterns are quite habitual and somewhat ingrained, this incorporation will take more than an intellectual awareness and a sincere desire, to make them your prime communication tools. Determined focus, diligent practice and objective feedback over an extended timeframe are necessary to get to the place where these communication tools can become second nature.

Victims Repel – Killing Off The Passive Voice

When you describe situations by using language that expresses what happened to you, you're taking on the role of a victim. If, instead, you can describe what happened, what the circumstances are, and what you're doing as a result of what happened, you will be able to experience the situation differently.

COMPARE:
    ✗ Victim Statement: "What happened to me just destroyed me."

    ✓ Situational Description: "The experience was so unpleasant and difficult."

so clinical & robotic

doesn't this run the risk of depersonalizing language & making it more difficult to connect w/ other people

COMPARE:

✗ Victim statement: "That kind of remark just does me in."

✓ Situational Description: "I experience that kind of remark in such a negative way. I like to make sure to discontinue communications when people speak that way."

sure, that sounds much more relateable 😊

COMPARE:

✗ Victim statement: "My wife dumped me for another man."

✓ Situational Description: "My wife decided she no longer wanted to be married to me."

just.... ew

COMPARE:

✗ Victim statement: "I was terminated and have to find a new job. "

✓ Situational Description: "My former employer eliminated my position and now I'm making decisions about what next career steps I want to make."

It's critical to become aware of how victim statements like these weaken how you feel about yourself and contribute to others seeing you defeated by your circumstances. By using situational descriptions instead, you will feel less like a victim and more in charge of your life, and those around you will see you in control of difficult challenges rather than as a powerless or injured person.

Losing a job often illustrates how people use victimized passive statements to describe their circumstances, conveying defenseless images of themselves:

- I got axed.
- I got fired.
- I was terminated.
- I got laid off.
- I was let go.

yes, when people go through painful experiences, we should use passionate language b/c we are not ROBOTS

What dreadful ways to describe an already difficult and painful experience! All of these statements are in the passive voice. Grammatically, the passive voice is when the action of the principal verb in the sentence is received by the subject of the sentence – rather than done by the subject of the sentence. Additionally, all of these sentences are victim statements. When one loses a job, it certainly does feel like control has been taken away; the sense of loss and helplessness can be quite strong. It's easy to fall into the trap of victimization. Selecting stronger active-voice sentences to describe a job termination will reduce that sense of loss and victimization a great deal.

Here are some ways of describing job loss without using the passive voice and without being a victim:

- "My company is going though a big downsizing, so I'm currently focusing on obtaining a new position as a ...."
- "I am making career decisions as a result of the elimination of my job."
- "When I left the XXX Company, I decided to look for a role in the ZZZ industry where I can bring my expertise in YYY."

I thought direct honesty was most important ...

While conducting a workshop for sales people for a major retailer that was closing one of its key branch locations, I gave a similar recommendation about avoiding passive victimized language. A workshop participant announced that she thought this advice was foolish. "Everyone knows the store is closing. I'm telling people I got laid off. Using this other type of description sounds contrived to me." One of her coworkers immediately chimed in to support my view-point, saying, "Well, I totally disagree with you. What would you rather say to people? I got screwed or I made love?" It certainly was a much cruder illustration of the point than I would ever have used in my workshop and yet I couldn't have been more pleased to have such a graphic way of demonstrating the benefit of eliminating passive, victim-ized, self-defeating language. *fundamentally flawed (it's no choice) analogy — more like rape*

It's about choosing active voice language that illustrates what you're doing or passive voice language that describes what's being done to you. One of the types of passive ex-pressions that I always challenge is the use of a form of the word "make" that expresses blame and lack of responsibil-ity for one's actions:

this I actually agree with

- "That **made** me so angry."
- "She **makes** me want to cry."
- "He **made** me lose control of what I was doing."
- "When you interrupt me, you **make** me forget what I'm saying."

Each one of these sentences gives up responsibility for self and blames someone or something outside of self for feel-ings and reactions. Let's eliminate "make" from each of these statements and look at non-passive, non-accusatory ways of expressing the exact same sentiments.

    ✗ "That **made** me so angry."
    ✓ "When that happens, I get so angry."

we can't always choose what happens to us but we can choose how we respond

✗ "She **makes** me want to cry."
✓ "When I listen to her, I feel like I want to cry."

✗ "He **made** me lose control of what I was doing."
✓ "Because I was so focused on what he said, I lost control of what I was doing."

✗ "When you interrupt me, you **make** me forget what I'm saying."
✓ "Whenever you interrupt me, I forget what I was just saying."

By adjusting the way you express yourself in this way, you will eliminate passivity, blame and victimization. You will benefit from how different it feels to make these types of statements and you will hear dramatically different types of responses from others.

THROW AWAY THAT CHISEL

It's always startling to hear confident and articulate people chiseling away at what they're describing by using limiting words and descriptors such as:

> **some, a little, probably, kind of, sort of, I think, I believe, only just, I guess**

COMPARE: *women are socialized to add qualifiers like this to personalized statements*

fact **AVOID:** "I have **some** experience in merchandising."
BETTER: "I have merchandising experience."

not fact **AVOID:** "I **think** my greatest strength is loyalty."
BETTER: "I see my greatest strength as loyalty."

I agree w/ removing qualifiers from objective facts but NOT from subjective statements & judgements

LOL not in engineering

not fact **AVOID:** "I **believe** I can get that done on time."
BETTER: "I'm confident I can get that done on time."

fact **AVOID:** "I've **only just** done that once before."
BETTER: "I've done that before."

fact **AVOID:** "I **sort of** want to do that."
BETTER: "I want to do that."

fact **AVOID:** "I **guess** I'd prefer chocolate ice cream."
BETTER: "I'd prefer chocolate ice cream."

not fact **AVOID:** "That would **probably** be a good idea."
BETTER: "That's a good idea."

The goal is to remove limiters from your communication without being arrogant or misrepresenting yourself in any way. Notice that in the recommended statements in the above comparisons, there's no exaggeration or enhancement of the basic fact conveyed in each of the preceding limited statements. *I don't think the author knows what a fact is*

When you use these types of limiting phrases, it's like taking a chisel and chipping away at what's solid in your life. The "only just", "sort of" syndrome can weaken everything you're saying, if you let it become a part of your everyday way of communicating.

once again, the author has some very valid points, but uses them in a black & white blanket manner rather than exploring any nuance

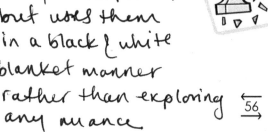

Another way people chip away at what they're saying is by starting sentences with qualifiers like "Although", "Even though", "In spite of", and "Despite". By beginning your comments like this, you put the focus on what's lacking, on the facet you most want to downplay. Compare the difference between beginning with this type of qualifier and beginning with the aspect you actually want to emphasize.

this is better be cause it highlights what needs to be focused on

AVOID: *NO* "**In spite** of how low our fundraising was this year, we have the largest membership we've ever had."

BETTER: "**We now have the largest membership base we've ever had and want to increase our fundraising to the same superlative level.**"

AVOID: *YES* "**Even though** I didn't buy you a birthday present, I'd like to take you out to dinner."

BETTER: "**I'd like to take you to dinner for your birthday.**"

AVOID: *YES* "**Although** there isn't any chocolate ice cream left, there's still plenty of vanilla".

BETTER: "**There's still plenty of vanilla ice cream left now that the chocolate is finished.**"

AVOID: *YES* "**Despite** how long it's taken me to do this research, I'm pleased with the findings I'm reporting."

BETTER: "**I'm pleased with the findings I'm reporting to you, after devoting in-depth time to collecting all of the required data.**"

People use these limiters and qualifiers mostly out of habit, often originally formed either from a lack of confidence or a desire to be seen as honest or modest. Again, we can contrast confidence to arrogance and arrogance to modest subservience, and can come to the conclusion that confidence is the winner over these other two character-istics. When a well-known State Senator with extensive ex-perience and expertise describes himself as just a simple country lawyer to disarm people or keep them from seeing his sense of superiority, that type of self-qualifier can have an undesirable negative impact, leaving people with an impression of false modesty or inflated self-esteem.

In addition to the lack of confidence (or ironic arrogance) these expressions convey, they also simply become fillers that dilute what you're saying. If you listen to the responses to most interview questions in the media, you will hear the vast majority of people start their answers with, "Well, I think ..." Those three words may possibly be the most frequently used words at the beginning of all interview responses. They, therefore, are hackneyed, overused words that lose their meaning and in addition to qualifying, they become the same as saying "um" to fill in dead space.

WHICH IS FINE

No More Buts

What would happen if you made a pact with yourself to go through an entire day without saying the word "but" a single time? It may be much harder than you think. For some reason, people have a tendency to get from one thought to the next through the use of this tiny word:

- "I like coffee **but** I like tea better."
- "London is a pretty city **but** Paris is more beautiful."
- "I'm going to a movie **but** I'd prefer to see a play."
- "New York has great architecture **but** Chicago's architecture is magnificent."

La autora creé que es una maestra, pero ella, en realidad, es una hack

And even:

- "What do you mean you're going home now? **But,** of course you'll come over for dinner."

So you see that "but" can be a useful word to connect thoughts and can be totally harmless or simply practical in a lot of what we say.

If you were to focus on artificially eliminating "but" across the board from your vocabulary, you'd become much more aware of the frequency and situations of how you use it. There are two particular instances when this tiny word becomes huge, powerful and <u>detrimental</u>:

I prefer the term gadfly

1. When someone becomes known as a "<u>yeah but</u>" person
2. When an individual negates all of <u>what he or she has just said by starting the next comment with BUT</u>

Beginning responses with "yeah but" will engender a reputation for being difficult, negative and argumentative. No matter what the "yeah but" person wants to convey or actually says, what people will tend to hear is:

- ✗ "Yeah but that will never work."
- ✗ "Yeah but that's a stupid idea."
- ✗ "Yeah but I disagree with you completely."
- ✗ "Yeah but I don't want to hear your views."

Instead of conveying:

   ✗ "Yeah but that will never work."

You can express yourself in this manner instead:

   ✓ "I hear what you want to do with the event tonight and here's what I see is the way to achieve the success you're looking for."

In Chapter Two, we saw that if you validate what people have said to you and follow your validation immediately with a disclaimer that begins with "but", you will have negated what you said in the prior validation statement. Also, you will have set the stage for argument rather than discussion:

   ✗ "I hear how much you want to go to Mexico over Christmas **but** I hate the hot weather and want to be where I can ski for the holidays."

   ✓ "I know that you want to go to Mexico where it is warm for the holidays. It's really important to me to be in a cooler climate and ski over Christmas."

By eliminating "but", you can create a natural progression to add another validation like:

   ✓ "Let's figure out how to plan our vacation time so that we both are happy with our choice."

Adjusting the words and tone of your communication to reflect a level playing field of communication without the "yeah but" disclaimer or the "but" negation will bring ease and enhancement to difficult conversations. Reminding yourself of the equal two-way street and the importance of validating people will also go a long way toward correcting the misuse and overuse of the word "but".

$\rightarrow$

Validation

$\leftarrow$

To break the pattern of frequently using the word "but" see how often you can end one sentence and start the next one without saying "but" or can substitute the word "and" in place of "but" whenever possible.

"New York has great architecture **but** Chicago's architecture is magnificent."

"New York has great architecture *and* Chicago's architecture is magnificent."

"New York has great architecture. Chicago's architecture is magnificent."

SAY IT WITHOUT THE NOT

For every comment that has the word "not" in it or is constructed in the negative, there's an affirmative way of saying exactly the same thought. Many people have a natural tendency to use the negative formation of sentences rather than the affirmative.

They prefer to say,

✗ "It isn't necessary to wash the dishes tonight."
rather than say,

✓ "It's okay to leave the dirty dishes until tomorrow."

They choose to say,

✗ "No problem, I don't mind at all."
rather than say,

✓ "Absolutely, I'd be delighted to do that."

being delighted is __not__ the same as not minding

Their first inclination is often to say,

    ✗ "That will never work."

rather than say,

    ✓ "Here's what will make that really successful."

LoL that is not the same thing

They start their sentences with

    ✗ "I don't think that ..."

rather than say,

    ✓ "My opinion is ..."

I agree it's best not to always use the negative form, but it is also better in some contexts

It's an extremely beneficial exercise to <u>become acutely aware of how often you use the negative form in communication</u> and to find a way to express exactly what you want to say using an affirmative form instead. Obviously, saying the words, "not" or "never" in your communications will be appropriate and acceptable in many instances. If, though, you can get yourself to be aware and challenge your use of negative expression, you will find that it's easy to switch to the affirmative and the value of making this switch is vast. It's always better to be thought of as a positive person rather than a negative one.

To begin to appreciate this value, reflect on the fact that one of the most common ways of expressing agreement is the response, "no problem" which is comprised of two negative words, one of which indicates difficulty. Rather than introduce such negative wording into a positive expression of agreement, it's certainly preferable to use affirmative words like "definitely", "with pleasure", "sure", or "absolutely" than to reply, "no problem" when you want to give an affirmative response.

no hay de que

Compare the following pairs of sentences:

AVOID: "I don't want to relocate to London."
BETTER: **"I want to live and work in San Francisco."**

AVOID: "I don't want to join the product team."
BETTER: **"I want to remain in the private banking group."**

AVOID: "No problem..."
BETTER: **"Absolutely, tell me more about it."**

AVOID: "I don't like it that you never include me in the planning meetings."
BETTER: **"I want you to know how much I'd like to participate in the planning meetings."**

AVOID: "Since I didn't have enough time this week, I won't be able to finish my report until next Friday. "
BETTER: **"Since I had unexpected commitments this week, I shifted priorities and will be able to finish my report by next Friday."**

AVOID: "I didn't realize how long it had been since we saw each other."
BETTER: **"How wonderful to spend time with you after all these years."**

Establish good language patterns by using affirmative sentence formation whenever possible. Avoid negative sentence construction and stay away from negative or confrontational language, even in the subtlest ways. So often people describe what they don't like or don't want to do rather than focus on what they like and do want to do. Describe what you want to *move toward* rather than what you want to *move away from*.

GETTING TO NEUTRAL

As we saw in Chapter One, with such a small window of opportunity to get the words right, it's critical to select words thoughtfully. Without realizing it, we can create a spark that can lead to a flame, by using words that invoke strong undesirable responses. Certain words convey much more than we intend or have an underlying meaning that can weaken or sabotage what we want to express, or, even worse, can provoke and agitate.

How we choose words can be powerful. Compare the following word pairs:

AVOID: Revolution *~ not the same*
BETTER: **Evolution** *—*

AVOID: Problem
BETTER: **Opportunity**

AVOID: Issue
BETTER: **Situation** *— doesn't situation sound worse?*

AVOID: Concern
BETTER: **Important Topic**

AVOID: Conflict *bahahaha*
BETTER: **Examination of Different Viewpoints**

AVOID: Negotiate
BETTER: **Talk About**

AVOID: Resolve
BETTER: **Reach Agreement**

AVOID: Change
BETTER: **Grow, Expand, Enhance**

Examine the following pairs of comments to see how selecting these types of recommended words can contribute to neutralizing potential conflict or to calming volatile or escalating emotions:

AVOID: "Let's sit down and negotiate where we're going with this issue."
BETTER: **"Let's sit down and _talk about_ where we're going with this _situation_."**

AVOID: "We have to get this conflict resolved."
BETTER: **"It's important for us to _examine all of the differing points of view_ and _reach agreement_ on this _important topic_."**

AVOID: "We have a problem that will require change."
BETTER: **"We have an _opportunity_ that will require _new growth and enhancement_."**

Look at the following two responses to see how subtly a word like "willing" affects what is being said:

    ✗ "We're <u>willing</u> to move our offices into the designated new space."
    ✓ "We're **_on board_** with moving our offices into the designated new space."

and what if that's exactly what you're trying to convey?

The first response subtly suggests that the speaker may not like this idea very much and is somewhat reluctant about it. The second response clearly shows alignment and agreement, regardless of whether the individual making that statement actually likes the idea of the move. Often people respond to

so a lie

a lot of these suggestions read as slapping an inauthentic veneer of business bullshit on → top of direct, honest conversation

a request by saying, "Yes, I'd be willing to do that." Without people realizing it, the use of the word "willing" in an affirmative response actually introduces the concept of doing something against their will or perhaps of feeling just a little bit begrudging. Certainly, there may be instances when it's appropriate or desirable to indicate that you're making a concession and the use of the word "willing" would reflect that well. If your goal is to convey positive agreement, avoid saying that you're willing to do something.

SAVE YOUR APOLOGIES *is she going to address the gendered elephant in the room?*
What reactions do you have when a person is always apologizing for everything? When someone over-apologizes, taking responsibility for all that is wrong in the universe, it wears thin, erasing any appreciation that would follow a sincere and appropriate apology. What comes to mind with an individual like this is the following communication symbol we looked at previously:

$$\nearrow | \swarrow$$

Constant apologizing tilts the playing field against you rather than wins people over. There's so much supplication and indication of guilt coming from this kind of repeated response that effectiveness in communication is lost. Certainly, if you've wronged someone or done something that you know is immoral or erroneous, an apology is exactly the right communication. Being sorry is about regret or penitence. If you say it constantly or mechanically, when the time comes for a real apology, no one will be listening or taking you seriously. Another reason to avoid saying you're sorry all the time is that "sorry" is also a synonym for "worthless", "contemptible", "dismal" or "gloomy".

or it can be as effective verbal subtle signaling

Instead of starting an immediate response with "Well, I think ..." to avoid silence, it would be better to leave a pause in front of your answer and even take a moment to reflect before you speak. Empty space around and within what you're saying provides emphasis and clarity and is a natural part of communication, just like the white space that adds so much to written communication. Speaking too fast is another way we fill every possible empty moment with sound to delete the valuable white space that adds meaning and enhances understanding.

After pointing out to a radio broadcast talk show host that she'd said "uh" thirty-six times in the opening four-minute segment of her show, she said, "That's very important to me. I will stop doing that." And yet the "uh" continued to salt-and-pepper her communication, both on air and off. Even seasoned communicators who have professional roles in Communication have difficulty breaking old habits.

These patterns are ingrained. I often recommend to people that they ask family members to snap their fingers or to signal through some pre-selected gesture every time they hear the hackneyed word or phrase that the individual wants to eliminate. Sometimes there is even a monetary fine that accumulates to stimulate attentiveness and correction. It certainly takes awareness and determination to get to where the new pattern is second nature.

why does she want everyone to sound exactly the same? how boring!

It's easy to fall into the repetition snare and use the same words or phrases over and over. It's a trap that's important to avoid. One of the best ways to recognize and overcome your communication challenges is to record yourself speaking to someone or making a presentation, so that you can recognize what your repetitive patterns are and decide what you want to adjust.

Whenever you use an expression, phrase or word repeatedly, what you say will be worn-out and lose meaning.

You Really Shouldn't "Should"
Four little words that can get you into great big trouble:

"I think you should..."

Life is full of paradox. Yes, people ask you for advice all the time. "So, what do you think I should do?" The truth is, however, they don't actually like your telling them what to do! Additionally, they don't like feeling judged. And most of all, as a result of telling people what they should do, you then

put yourself in the undesirable position of sharing responsibility for other people's choices. So, given these givens,
what would contribute to your wanting to tell others what
they should do?

haha not this bitch

Interestingly, when I ask people if they have a desire to tell
others what to do, they usually answer that they don't. So
the question remains. What causes people to say so often
to others, "I think you should..."?

This is a good time to look back once again at our validation two-way street symbol:

→

Validation

←

ohhhh, I get it now, the author comes from money, which explains her privileged views

When people ask you what you think they should do, they
usually want most of all to hear you validate what they have
been telling you. Instead of saying:

> ✗ "I think you should buy the $750.00 pair of boots be-
> cause you have worked hard for your money and
> you deserve those boots."

OR:

> ✗ "I think you shouldn't buy the $750.00 pair of boots
> because you have worked so hard for your money
> that it would be extravagant and disrespectful to
> spend that much money on a pair of boots."

A better choice would be to say something like:

> ✓ "I can see how much you want the $750 pair of
> boots and I know how hard you work to earn the

money to be able to afford to buy them. It sounds like you're really torn about spending that kind of money for a pair of boots. What's going to feel better to you: spending that much money on those boots because you want them so much or buying a cheaper pair that you like less that saves you several hundred dollars?"

Even when we have the authority and responsibility to tell others what to do, "should" sets a tone that generates resistance and pushback:

✗ "You should have been in bed hours ago."

✗ "You should have presented me with these numbers on Monday before today's meeting took place so that I'd have been prepared."

✗ "You should have finished your homework this afternoon so that you could go with us to the movies."

✗ "You should have told me that you wanted to take this fishing trip to Alaska in August at the beginning of the summer before I scheduled vacations."

✗ "You should have known better than to do that."

These statements are all expressions of legitimate authority. What's wrong with them is that their principal sentiment is judgment rather than authority. When you judge someone, you undermine your own authority and you generate responses full of hostility, animosity, defensiveness or resistance. In communicating judgment, you're talking down to the other person and immediately tilt the equal two-way street of communication to look like this:

These five statements contain blame without expressing the reaction or feeling of the speaker in a direct manner. Their tone is threatening yet they don't indicate any repercussions for the behavior that's being judged. So many people in positions of authority – parents and managers – become so frustrated with the behavior of their children or their subordinates and so insecure about their own authority that they lash out and attack rather than express their reactions, wants and subsequent actions clearly and directly.

One of my closest friends since childhood has eight sons. It's amazing to have been in their home many times over the years and never have heard one disrespectful word from these boys to their mother. There's a simple reason for this. She always talks to them on her own level in this manner:

She also always validates them, respectfully, when she asserts her authority:

Validation

She has authority and they respect her. I've heard her refuse to allow them to do what they want to do. I've heard her tell them that she can't give them what they're asking her for. I've even asked her if the behavior I've seen over the years is for my benefit and when I'm not in the house if there's a totally different interaction between her sons and her. She's confirmed that what I've observed is the way it's always been in her home. She's never talked down to her children and as a result, she's earned their respect and they naturally demonstrate that all the time.

Let's return to our previous five "should" sentences and look at different ways to express reactions to the same situations with authority, confidently, directly, without judgment, and without saying "should":

✓ "We agreed that your bedtime is 9:00 PM and it's now 11:00 and you're still up. I'm disappointed that this keeps happening. Since you haven't kept our agreement, I've decided to take away your XXX privileges until you can get to bed on time for (amount of) days."

✓ "I know you've been swamped in the last week and as much as I understand that, I'm still extremely concerned that I didn't get the numbers I needed from you by Monday for today's meeting. Here's what I want to see going forward to avoid this kind of situation from happening again. ...."

✓ "I see how unhappy you are that we're going to the movies without you because you haven't finished your homework. I hope you'll be able to go with us next week. I'd be happy to sit down together with you tomorrow and look at ways for you to use your time differently."

✓ "That trip to Alaska sounds fabulous and I hear how important it is to you. It's too late now for me to change the vacation schedule. I wish you'd given me more advanced notice. I'm asking you to give me at least two months' notice for any vacation request going forward."

✓ "Since we've talked about this so many times, I'm surprised to see that you've done that again."

When your goal **is** to advise someone in a specific way or to express to others what you see as the correct choice, there is an excellent way to communicate your recommendation and/or authority without telling anyone what they *should* do:

AVOID SAYING:

✗ "Here's what I think you should do."

INSTEAD SAY:

✓ "Here's what I think is most important to consider."

AVOID SAYING:

✗ "Here's what you should do to fix this."

INSTEAD SAY:

✓ "Here's what I see as the best solutions to this."

There's a subtle and important difference in both of these pairs of communication options. In each of the first statements, you're participating in the choice, putting pressure on the other person, or stating an expectation. In both of the second statements, you're taking responsibility for your opinion and removing yourself from the actual decision that only the other person can make. What we think is right for another person may be quite different from what the other person believes or wants.

"don't participate in their choice"

Another type of "should" is the one we direct toward ourselves in a reprimanding way:

    ✗ "I should have told you."
    ✗ "I should have done more."
    ✗ "I shouldn't have eaten that."

When you start your thoughts with the words, "I should" (or shouldn't), you're blaming yourself and assuming guilt, without taking real responsibility for your actions and choices. There's a helpless guilt that accompanies seeing and expressing yourself this way. The excuse is given, the shame is attached and the decision to act differently going forward is buried or ignored.

It takes courage and awareness to say instead:

    ✓ "I know you're hurt that you learned about this from someone other than me. I feel bad that I didn't tell you myself."
    ✓ "I see how much more time I could have given and I wish that I had. Going forward I want to look at my priorities and make time for what is important."
    ✓ "I'm aware that I'm over-eating and eating foods that are not good for me. It's important to me to change my eating habits."

By expressing yourself in this fuller way, you're facing what's underneath the "I should" words. Heaping guilt on yourself is non-productive and unhealthy. Using the word "should" to absolve yourself of guilt is also undesirable. When you work on addressing the use of self-directed "shoulds", you come face to face with your own desires, your level of motivation and most importantly your ability to be self-accepting and tolerant. If you can't be tolerant of yourself, it's unlikely you will be tolerant of others.

As soon as you remove the word "should" from your communications and express your reactions and wishes without judgment, you will start to find better ways to speak to people, will feel differently when you're speaking to them and, best of all, will also get better responses in return.

ADJUST YOUR JARGON

Just because you know what the initials you're saying stand for, doesn't mean that everyone else does. When terms are used so frequently, they become part of your everyday vocabulary and it's easy to forget that others don't understand their meaning.

When I was having dinner at a neighbor's, another guest mentioned that his son was in HVAC. He said it, thinking that everyone else at the table knew what that was. I didn't, so I asked him. He told me it meant Heating, Ventilation and Air Conditioning, and looked at me in a strange way as if surprised I didn't know what those letters stood for.

In a conversation with a colleague, I was shocked to hear him say that someone had ask him what an MSW was (Masters in Social Work) since this designation was so familiar to me. I hadn't even thought of the possibility of its sounding like jargon to someone.

Jargon excludes people, inhibits understanding and can have three meanings that are highly undesirable:

1. Verbal communication that's confusing and unclear
2. The special language of a specific activity or group
3. Obscure and pretentious language

I also worry about the opposite – if I assume my audience doesn't know certain things, so I spell them out, I don't want to come across as underestimating their intelligence & knowledge

In the workplace there are so many acronyms and terms that people become accustomed to using, they forget that others don't know what they mean. It's quite off-putting to hear someone talking as if the entire world understands what he or she is saying, when in fact most people don't. The dislike for this type of communication has given birth to terms like legalese and psychobabble.

Many environments and activities have their own terms that people generally aren't familiar with. If a sailor asks another sailor to trim the jib, there will be an immediate understanding of what to do; yet an instruction like that will feel like a foreign language to a non-sailor.

There's also the tendency to think in certain settings it's necessary to use language that is appropriate for that situation. While it's certainly good to differentiate between the way you talk in a leisure setting and a work or business setting, avoid using jargon or sounding artificial or stilted in those more formal settings.

I'm always amazed at the sudden transformation that takes place when I coach people who are preparing for job interviews. Even though I recommend that people be highly selective in what they say on job interviews, I feel sad and surprised when I see wonderful, interesting people I know and enjoy having a conversation with, disappear and become wooden and strange as soon as they begin to answer job interview questions. They often use peculiar jargon or trite language that I never hear them using in other types of communication. I no longer recognize them. "Growth", "challenge", "opportunity", "that would allow me to", "blah, blah, blah" ... I want to say, "Where did you go?" "Who are you?" "What are you talking about?" The key is to sound natural and conversational and to use the same language you would use in a normal everyday conversation.

It's a good practice to be sure that the language you're using is common language, familiar to everyone.

REPLACE NEEDY WITH WHOLE

There's an unrecognized phenomenon that underlies the cause for people to feel they don't have the right to express how they're making choices. As a result, people say they **have** to do a certain task or they **can't** do something, rather than say they're choosing one option over another. Often children will tell us they **can't help** doing what they're doing. If they're using phrases like this, they've learned that way of expressing their frustration from someone, somewhere. As adults, when we say, "I can't help it." or "I can't do XXX." what we're usually experiencing is frustration, challenge or difficulty rather than actual inability. We will feel much less helpless about life's challenges if we replace "can't" with wording that is more in sync with reality. Rather than say "I can't", we can say:

✓ "This is difficult to do."
✓ "I'm finding it very frustrating to do this."
✓ "I see XXX as a big challenge."

Another way we push ourselves around and get caught in a trap of our own making is when we say, "I have no choice." about a situation. We may feel like there's no way out or that our obligations are so strong they negate other options. It's still better to say, "Based on the strong sense of responsibility I feel about this, I'm making the choice to stay involved." When we say we have no choice, we're denying or fighting our responsibility and our choice on some level.

this I agree w/ completely — there's ALWAYS a choice

What we are looking at is how:

- ✗ People let language become a crutch they use to relinquish responsibility and shift it onto some unknown force.
- ✗ Feelings of guilt and insecurity sneak into language patterns and become habitual.
- ✗ Needy syndromes can infiltrate our communication, acting as barriers to feeling whole.

To recognize all of this more clearly, let's compare two different ways of communicating choices:

AVOID: "I **can't** go with you to the concert because I **have** to go to a lecture with my brother-in law. Thanks for asking me."

BETTER: **"I would like to go to the concert with you. I promised my brother-in-law that I would go to a lecture with him and am going to keep my commitment. Thanks for asking me."**

AVOID: "I **can't** go to dinner tonight because I **have** to do my laundry."

BETTER: **"I want to do my laundry tonight so I've decided to stay in rather than go out to dinner."**

LoL, no one wants to do laundry

AVOID: "As a payroll supervisor, I **have** to make certain that all checks have been properly reconciled."

BETTER: **"As a payroll supervisor, I'm in charge of making certain that all checks have been reconciled."**

AVOID: "I **can't** drive a car in Manhattan.

BETTER: **"Since I have only driven a car in Ohio where I grew up, I'm afraid to drive a car in New York City."**

AVOID: "I **have no choice** about this decision. I'm **stuck with** this until the end."

BETTER: **"Since I've invested so much time in this project and care about it deeply, I've decided to stick it out until the end even though I have a sour taste in my mouth related to what has just occurred."**

Neediness in language is self-defeating, weak and most often *weird* inaccurate. An amusing saying grew out of the Women's *capitalization* movement: "A woman needs a man like a fish needs a bi- *zation* cycle." In the world today, many people are choosing a *choice* variety of alternate lifestyles that would certainly validate this statement. The importance of the statement, from a communication standpoint, is how well it demonstrates the distinction between desire and requirement. So often we confuse the two.

Compare two different ways of expressing the same desire:

- "Without a spouse, my life is incomplete."
- "I want a partner to share and enrich my life."

"I'm trying" is another speech pattern that demonstrates lack rather than gain. Even though making an effort by try-ing is certainly preferable to whining or sitting on your back-side, the words themselves indicate deficiency rather than attainment. Think how much better it sounds to say, "My goal is to finish writing this section of my report by Friday." than to say, "I'm trying to finish my report by Friday." Also it is much better to tell someone, "I want to be able to under-stand what you're telling me." rather than say, "I'm trying to understand what you're saying."

The communication paths away from neediness and into wholeness are:

AVOID: "I have to ..."
BETTER: "I want to ..."

AVOID: "I can't ..."
BETTER: "This is difficult to do."

AVOID: "I need ..."
BETTER: "I would like ..."

AVOID: "I have no choice."
BETTER: "I have decided that ..."

AVOID: "I'm trying to ..."
BETTER: "My goal is to ..."

Speak Easy Rules

Review and Summary:

4 | Replacing Deadly Habits

✓ Avoid passive or victimized language.

✓ Express yourself in the affirmative.

✓ Choose neutral rather than negatively-charged words.

✓ Recognize the pitfalls of giving people advice.

✓ Eliminate hackneyed ways of communicating.

again, this section is very strongly
rooted in a very specific cultural
class & strips humanity & color out of
language — it also devalues
female modes of communication in favor
of male

she does make some decent points
about "needy" language & jargon

Speak Easy:
The Human Side

5 | Be Your Own Best Friend

As we continue on this communication voyage together, it's important for us to remember that the personal side of communication runs deep. We all bring baggage and history to every exchange we have, most of which remains on an unconscious level yet always has an influence.

Since so much of how we receive communication is non-verbal - with the largest portions coming from facial expression and tone of voice – it's very tricky to disconnect our emotions from the reactions we have to what people say to us. We can gain meaningful insight into how we interpret what people say, and into our subsequent feelings and reactions, from looking again at that large percentage of non-verbal communication from Chapter Two.

How Communication Is Received:

**Non-verbal
93%**   **Verbal
7%**

Our underlying attitudes and judgments add so much to what we communicate and to how our communications are received. Starting with self-awareness, we can open our eyes and bring a new sensitivity to how we interact with people. Additionally, we will want to examine the risks involved in communicating in new ways.

It's up to each of us:

     ✓ To adjust how we experience and respond to negativity around us
     ✓ To be the primary source of our own well-being
     ✓ To be our own best friend

And we must do these **without**:

     ✗ Acquiescing to abusive power
     ✗ Condoning inappropriate communication
     ✗ Thinking it's easy to ignore negative communication and behavior

achieving these things is a constant goal, must always be on your toes

Life Is Hard – Easy Is As Easy Says

Let's remember the childhood saying, "Sticks and stones can break your bones but words can never hurt you." so that we can become stronger and stay intact when we experience negative emotions or reactions in response to what someone has said to us.

Over the years, I've heard a wide variety of reactions to situations in the workplace.
Person A will say,

> "I'm so used to hearing my boss, Grace, fly off the handle like that. I just ignore her. She always calms down eventually and sometimes she even apologizes. I know it's more about her frustration than it is about me, even though she directs such hostility towards me sometimes. She's really pathetic that way. The main thing for me is that I feel good about myself and my work. I really love what I do here and I wouldn't let her bad behavior change that for a second. I'd be happier if she'd calm down and stop attacking everybody. It would be better for the company too."

Person B, in the same setting with a similar job and an exactly parallel relationship to that manager, will have a completely different experience of the same type of communications from the manager and say,

> "No matter what we do, Grace is never happy with our work. Some

days I can barely get myself to come in to the office; I never know if it's going to be a horrible day because she's in such a frenzy and will make me crazy and depressed. I just don't think I can listen to her attack me the way she does anymore. I hate having a boss who is constantly criticizing me like that. I'll probably leave the company before the end of the year because of how she treats me."

What gives **Person A** the ability to separate herself from the attack of her boss? She clearly gets the "sticks and stones break bones and words never hurt you" message. What comes first for **Person A** is her own self-esteem which is closely aligned with her focus on and enjoyment of work. She also disconnects her boss's erratic attacking behavior from herself, by seeing it as generalized rather than targeted at her.

Person B has a much more personal experience of what his manager says to him. His self-esteem suffers and he lets his manager completely obliterate his ability to focus on anything other than how destroyed and distraught he is because of his boss's constant criticism. He's a defeated victim and his work-life is a picture of total stress because of his boss.

If we could gain some distance and perspective to examine the whole of our individual lives from beginning to end, surely the importance of a single person's negative behavior, in the grand scheme of who we are, would take on an entirely new perspective and be relatively insignificant. When we give others the power to destroy our well-being and our ability to communicate effectively, we're actually feeding the monster.

so where is the balance?
don't let the manager get to you personally, but still advise her (or HR) of the toxic work environment she's creating?

it still takes energy to deal w/ a negative person, even if that energy is spent not letting them get to you

This is similar to Franklin D. Roosevelt's quote, "The only thing we have to fear is fear, itself." People can't terrorize you verbally without your participation on some level. Here are some suggested ways of responding to inappropriate, out of line, aggressive communication:

even if that "participation" is to stay silent?

"I hear how concerned you are about XXX and am happy to look at ways to improve this situation. I want to talk to you about this later (or: tomorrow, at another time, this afternoon, etc.) when you're calm and when you can talk to me in a different and respectful way."

~~~

"I want to have this conversation when my own feelings and reactions to what you've just said are on a more even keel."

~~~

"I respect your viewpoint and recognize that you're absolutely clear and firm about how you see this. I will not have a conversation with anyone who talks to me the way you're speaking right now."

There are potential risks in standing up for and asserting your-self like this. You must feel strong and confident to respond to people in this manner. The most likely outcome, however, will be a new found self-respect and respect from the other person, as well as new self-awareness that will <u>change the dynamics of future dialogues.</u> quite the optimist, this author

When responding in this new way, it's crucial that you incor-porate the basic principles of validation and the two-way street of level communication. When emotions run high, it's hard for you to know whether you're actually speaking to another person in a neutral, mutually respectful, level tone and whether your facial expression is free from revealing emotion that contradicts the words you're saying.

Validation

Three critical human factors are interwoven in the mix when we first communicate in new ways:

1. Our intention may be different from our execution.
2. Others may be threatened or uncomfortable with the deviation from our typical pattern and style of commu-nicating – or from our habitually saying nothing. There could be a wide range of reactions as a result.
3. If the <u>person on the other side of the equation is men-tally unhealthy, "all bets are off"</u>. The response could even be hostile or physically aggressive.

this is why giving a mentally unstable narcisist the bully pulpit is a bad idea

When we stand up for ourselves, confidently, directly, and always respectfully without judgment, the risks of potential negative reactions are almost always worth the rewards, starting with your own sense of satisfaction for having stood up for yourself, appropriately.

What often occurs is people let fear and self-doubt keep them from saying what's important to them. If we always show respect for the other person's views and make sure we never come from a defensive or aggressive place, there will always be a good way to express our viewpoint and communicate our position.

except for when those positions will get you fired by your corporate overlords

Here are some questions to ask yourself prior to risking communication in difficult situations:

- ✓ "Am I taking this too personally and feeling unnecessarily put down or is this an abusive interaction that's nurtured by my victimized behavior where I continue to be a silent doormat?"

- ✓ "Who can I discuss this situation with in complete confidence to get another read on what's going on to validate my thinking and approach?"

- ✓ "Have I rehearsed what I'm going to say to gain self-confidence and get objective feedback to make sure that what I intend to say and how I'm saying it are in sync with my goals and with the likely outcomes of my communication?"

- ✓ "How well do I know the person I will speak to and how familiar am I with the typical reactions this individual will have to what I'm saying? Who can help me assess this realistically and confidentially?"

Self-Approval Is The Goal

The more dependent you are on getting approval and recognition from others so you can feel good about yourself, the more likely it will be that you will lose your sense of well-being in life without external reinforcement. Everyone thrives on praise. In the feedback I collect about managers that describes what they most need to change, a frequent response is the request to hear more praise. Wanting recognition for good work is a healthy desire yet quite different from being dependent on praise to gain a strong sense of self and to obtain satisfaction in life, which is a formula for disappointment and disaster.

Wanting Recognition = Healthy Desire

Dependence on Praise = Formula for Disaster

Feeling good about yourself and what you do is the primary key. This requires communicating your passion and dedication rather than depending on praise and reinforcement from others to validate who you are.

WELL-BEING

 =

FEELING GOOD ABOUT YOURSELF

Loss Is A Teacher

For many people, a major communication deficit is the ability to face and talk about loss. Ernest Hemingway wrote, "Life breaks everyone and some become strong in the broken places." In the play, *The Fantasticks*, there are these lyrics, "Without a hurt, the heart is hollow." Loss is certainly a

grit   • traumatropism

• Kintsugi

94

great teacher. What's most precious to us is what we can lose most easily or what's hardest to protect from loss. Loss is a natural outcome of living and it's how we cope with it and how we see it that can be the source of our strength and the basis for developing the ability to master life's challenges. Since loss is inevitable, the more we can learn to focus on and communicate the gains that come from loss, the more we will experience loss in ways that are manageable and life enriching.

There are many factors over which we have no control. We do, though, always have control over our perspectives and what we say to reflect them. The goal is to deal with what you face head on and to say what you want directly, rather than resort to being an ostrich.

The more you can talk about loss, using language that reflects what you've gained from what's missing, the easier it will be to experience loss in a powerful, learning, and full-of-growth way.

The most striking example to illustrate this communication shift for me occurred in 2001, shortly after 9/11 in New York City. I was walking through Bryant Park on a glorious autumn day. Giant white cloud-puffs floated in the brilliant blue sky behind the gleaming surrounding skyscrapers. I had been experiencing severe grief over the senseless destruction and needless sacrifice of life that had occurred a few weeks before. Like many New Yorkers, I'd been living with an enormous weight that I carried everywhere. It had kept me terrorized reclusively within a tiny radius of blocks from my home and office. Every communication I had, focused on my unbearable sense of loss. I had only just begun to venture beyond my fabricated self-designated safe zone.

Suddenly, a recognition and feeling of gratitude came over me. I felt grateful to be alive, to see the magnificence of my city, to know how precious life is, to recommit myself to making a difference in the world, to be able to give back for all that I had. I saw the world as inviting again rather than terrifying. Strangest of all, I felt gratitude to the terrorists for providing an unthinkable way for me to gain such deep appreciation. I knew that if I could go back in time, change history and pluck those airplanes from the sky, I'd have waved that life-saving magic wand in less than an instant. Somehow I'd found a way to see and communicate the beauty of what I'd lost and the magnificence of what I'd gained from loss.

Without painful and extraordinary loss, we can never value and see what we have in such a deep way. I've made dramatic choices in my life that often astound people. To me these valiant but simple choices reflect what I've learned from loss. Loss is our best teacher. "Without a loss, the heart is hollow."

Here are contrasting ways to speak about life situations that demonstrate how you can adjust your perspectives and the way you communicate regarding loss:

- ✗ "Without my wife of fifty-three years, life's not worth getting out of bed each day."
- ✓ "The memory of my wife of fifty-three years gives me renewed strength to tackle life every day."

- ✗ "I'll never do that again, after all that I lost the last time I tried it."
- ✓ "The next time I do that, I'll know a lot more about how to go about it, based on what I've learned from my previous experience and loss."

- ✗ "Now that I no longer have a mentor to guide me, I feel so lost."
- ✓ "With all I gained from my mentor who is no longer here, I have many great teachings to draw from and use as guides to the present and future."

Looking at life from a different perspective and finding language to reflect that perspective is the goal of choice. The more you shift perspectives about loss to perspectives of gain and use language that demonstrates the new views, the more successful your communications will be and the better you will feel about yourself and what you have to say.

Look In The Mirror – There's Got To Be A Pony Somewhere

Often when we look in the mirror of our lives, our view is narrow and distorted rather than broad and encompassing. There's a tendency for people to zero in on what's wrong or missing rather than see what they have. They also tend to bring a habitual optimistic or pessimistic perspective to their communications. Just like certain people have a tendency to use negative rather than affirmative language formation, people have a propensity to see the world from a full or empty perspective.

There's an often-told story of twin children with completely opposite views of the world - one was extremely optimistic and the other was quite far beyond pessimistic.

One Christmas Eve, their parents decided to take action to resolve their children's extreme views. The parents filled the little pessimist's room with every imaginable toy a child could want. They filled the little optimist's room with manure.

On Christmas morning, the parents first went to their pessimistic child's room to find the child crying in a heap in the middle of the room, lamenting, "With all these toys I got for Christmas, there are too many parts that can get broken. I'll never have enough batteries to keep these toys running. I won't be able to understand the instructions and learn how to use them. I'm probably too stupid to do them right anyway. I know I'm going to break something. Somebody will want to take these away from me. I'm going to have to share these with other kids. I don't know what to do first."

With sighs of exasperation, the parents left the pessimistic child's room and entered into the little optimist's room full of excrement. This second child was ecstatic and was running around screaming with joyful delight, "I am so excited. With what I woke up to in my room today, there's got to be a pony in here somewhere!"

It's definitely all about perspective. How you see the world becomes your reality and controls what you say about it.

QUENCHING YOUR THIRST NO MATTER WHAT'S IN THE GLASS
We know that over 90% of how we receive communication is non-verbal. Changing the words we use, however, still has the power to change how we feel and how others react to what we say. We will begin to see situations differently when we begin to choose different words to describe them:

    ✗ "There's only half a glass left."
    ✓ "There's still half a glass left."

    ✗ "She never calls me."
    ✓ "I'd like to talk to her more often."

✗ "At my age, there are so few options left for me."
✓ "At my age, I'm so clear about which options I want to select."

It's true that in many instances there's a smaller amount rather than a larger one to express in our communication. Rather than being about how full or empty the glass is, it's about explaining what there is in the glass to drink. If there are only three drops of water in the glass, the point is to figure out how to describe quenching your thirst with whatever amount you have. You can't articulate how to drink the empty part so it's unproductive to focus on it.

SEEKING SUPPORT: CUSHIONS HELP

So often, we're much harder on ourselves than others are on us. Rather than beat up on yourself, feed your guilt, or be a martyr; turn to others to gain support and perspective and to have a sounding board for your communications. You will frequently hear people describing their biggest challenges this way, "I could've never gotten through this without the help of others."

Seeking support is better than going it alone. Recognize, though, that when you seek the backing, comfort and counsel of friends, family members and coworkers, you can also be building a case and fueling the fire. It's clearly beneficial to ask for input from others about the way you're communicating in challenging situations and to have an ear to listen. In tough times, there's nothing more valuable than having a support system around you. If you don't already have people that you turn to, rethink your views and practices, and build a strong support network for the good times and the bad.

Being able to turn to others to share your story or even just to unload can be advantageous and satisfying. Make sure you include people outside of the actual setting or situation to do this with and make sure you're choosing people that you know you can trust for confidentiality. The benefit is to gain awareness and ease your heavy feelings. If your goal in bringing others into the picture is to vindicate yourself, add fuel to the fire, or defend your position, think carefully about what you're choosing to say. If the outcome is escalation of an already tense situation or further pressure for you or others, then seeking support will be self-defeating and only add to your challenge.

The best type of support is objective. The less involved the person is with your story, the more able that person will be to listen and respond without bias and concern for personal repercussions. A natural instinct of someone connected to you personally is to come to your defense and to say what you want to hear. Cushions like that feel wonderful to sink into; just make sure there are also those in your support mix that are free from wanting to please you or protect their own self-interests.

sometimes you need a cushion and sometimes you need a wood bench — harder to sit on, but still supportive

you don't want people who bolster your self-delusions

There's a good reason why people choose professional counsel and why professionals, like attorneys and psychologists, remove themselves from situations that can be seen as having conflicts of interest. Give yourself the cushion of support and choose supporters who can listen and respond as objectively as possible. Find people who will give you candid feedback and who can critique your communications and your strategies.

All that being said about objectivity and professional input, never underestimate the value of a good hug. To survive infancy, babies must be stroked and held. The human need for connection is universal. Enrich your life with balance and surround yourself with an array of support cushions. Take initiative, be responsible for yourself, seek input from others and make connections.

Never underestimate the value of a good hug!

Speak Easy Rules

Review and Summary:

5 | Be Your Own Best Friend

✓ Get your sense of well-being from yourself.

✓ Disempower abusive communicators.

✓ Focus on what you have rather than on what is missing.

✓ Value the gains you receive from loss.

✓ Build strong systems of support.

6 | Every Style Can Be Successful

When I see people express frustration when they watch others slide through life without friction, I'm quite sympathetic. How is it that for some people, the right words roll off of their tongues and it seems that everything falls in their laps effortlessly while others, even after lots of struggle, seem to end up a step away from where they intended to be and express themselves with neither grace nor ease?

First of all, life is random. I heard someone ask once, "Hasn't our family had its quota of suffering?" Alas, life works without a quota system, yet there are ways to enhance the odds of getting what you want and avoiding turmoil. You can influence how others see you and respond to you; you can't impose your standards on other people. You can adjust your perspective and you can adjust the way you communicate; you can't change people to match your view of how they should be. Rather than wanting to be like someone else, you can capitalize on your own style, strengths and preferences. A good first step is to become more self-aware.

Initiator Versus Responder

One of the most widely used personality assessment tools is The Myers Briggs Type Indicator (MBTI), a wonderful and multi-layered vehicle for developing self-understanding, for gaining tolerance and understanding of others, and for enhancing communication. The MBTI has earned its popularity by defining and reinforcing a range of distinct components of basic human personality styles.

> this is a problematic test that was not created based on extensive research

The MBTI bases its measurements on Jungian personality preferences. One element that Carl Jung identified, and the MBTI measures, is the flow of energy which Jung labeled as Introversion (having an inner directed flow of energy) or as Extraversion (having an outer directed flow of energy). While all of the many aspects of the MBTI have an impact on communication, the Introversion/Extraversion designation has the biggest and that's why I've chosen to focus only on this single dimension of the MBTI.

Two key characteristics distinguish the difference between Jung's definition of Introversion and Extraversion:

- Introverted people prefer to *respond* to others.
- Extraverted people prefer to *initiate* communications with others.

Extraverted people are credited with being outgoing because of their ease in reaching out and initiating contact. In the world of work and in the world of play, they're known for getting things rolling and for engaging others. The downside of being seen that way is that others can also see extraverted people as superficial or invasive.

What occurs in contrast is that introverted people, who prefer to respond rather than initiate, can be seen as aloof, shy, standoffish or lacking drive. Their upside is they're usually seen as deep and responsive.

This basic component of *"Initiator versus Responder"* greatly influences how people communicate and, as a result, how they are perceived by others.

Here are two contrasting checklists for the Initiator and the Responder to help you identify which type is more like you.

Typical traits of an *Initiator:*	Typical traits of a *Responder:*
☐ Likes to reach out to others	☐ Enjoys being receptive to others
☐ Initiates contact easily	☐ Respectful of the privacy of others
☐ Seen as outgoing	☐ Known for responsiveness
☐ Comfortable being in the spotlight	☐ Prefers being in the background
☐ Moves easily from topic to topic	☐ Gives deep attention to interest area
☐ Expressive	☐ Reflective
☐ Maintains eye contact to connect	☐ Breaks eye contact to consider

You may find that you've checked a number of boxes in both columns and that in different situations your tendencies and inclinations change. Even though the difference between being an Initiator and a Responder is striking, and is one of the most distinguishing characteristics of human dynamics, there are certainly a variety of variations on these two distinct and contrasting themes.

DIFFERENT APPROACHES FOR DIFFERENT STYLES
What's most helpful is to be aware of how these preferences influence the way you express yourself and to find natural and comfortable ways to communicate that match who you are.

Step One: Know what your preferences are.

Step Two: Look at ways to leverage what works best for you.

Step Three: Develop balance by expanding your repertoire.

Let's apply these three steps for the Initiator and the Responder to see how different styles can be effective:

Situation: *Pat has just moved into a new community and wants to meet/find people to play tennis with.*

Initiator Pat:
- **Step One:** Self-Awareness: **Likes to initiate speaking to strangers first.**

- **Step Two:** Comfort Zone: Walks into store two blocks from new home and says to owner, **"My name is Pat and I'm new here and would like to meet tennis players who live close by."**

- **Step Three:** Expanding Natural Repertoire: Uses telephone directory and Internet to find names of area sports facilities. Provides a written communication via email or bulletin board with name and phone number for people to call for tennis games. **Responds to email or telephone calls from others.**

Responder Pat
- **Step One:** Self-Awareness: **Prefers responding to others.**

- **Step Two:** Comfort Zone: Uses telephone directory and Internet to find names of area sports facilities. Provides a written communication via email or bulletin board with name and phone number for people to call for tennis games. **Responds to email or returns telephone calls from others.**

Step Three: Expanding Natural Repertoire: Walks into store two blocks from new home and says to owner, **"My name is Pat and I'm new here and would like to meet tennis players who live close by."**

FIGURING OUT WHAT WORKS FOR YOU

Rather than look to others to be more like they are, it's always better to look at how to be yourself in the way that works best for you. If you're self-aware, you can begin to examine how your style of communication can affect outcomes and reactions. Authenticity is the most critical part of every communication. If you're faking what you're saying or being mechanical in any way, you will feel inauthentic and, because of the large portion of communication that is non-verbal, others will sense that you lack sincerity.

There seems to be a paradox in this advice: How can you know and be true to yourself and also use communication approaches that are exactly the opposite of what feels most natural to you? If you start with self-awareness and hone your preferred style, you can think of expanding and stretching your natural base to acquire new approaches without abandoning what works best for you and without believing that you have to change to be more like someone else. It's about growth and expansion rather than about change and abandonment.

THE NEW STRESS EQUATION – IT'S ALL ABOUT HOW YOU SEE IT

We're so often limited by our narrow vision of a situation. Living in a tunnel prevents a view from other directions. Feelings are always legitimate; it's using feelings and reactions to keep you from seeing other perspectives that creates the most stress. The bigger view you have and the more you can recognize what others are seeing around you that's different from your view, the more you will be able to diminish the negative effects of stress and its harsh impact on how you communicate.

Recognizing that stress is a natural and required part of living will also add to your gaining perspective. To expand your known comfort zone requires stress. This applies to all facets of life and includes the most positive to the most negative life situations. Getting married, becoming a parent, starting a new job, are all joyful occasions, yet are also tremendous stress points in life. Of course, what becomes the biggest benefit in the stress that comes from expanding your known and comfortable world is the larger playing field you gain with a greater expanded comfort zone and a greater ease in your communications.

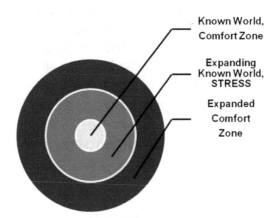

Known World,
Comfort Zone

Expanding
Known World,
STRESS

Expanded
Comfort
Zone

You can integrate stress into your life in a positive way and can diminish its harmful effects by following these basic simple guidelines:

 ✓ Remember that stress is a natural phenomenon of being alive.

✓ Gain perspective on the positive value of stress to stimulate new awareness.

✓ Look beyond your own stress points to see other perspectives. First the new perspective, then the new communication to reflect the bigger perspective; it's all about changing the view and fine-tuning the words.

Compare two different ways of seeing and describing the same situations:

AVOID: "Everything is coming in on me and there are so many major challenges right now that I don't even have time to think about addressing problems that come up on a day-to-day basis."

BETTER: **"Because the demands are so high, I want to look at all the angles and get all of the help possible to stay effective in such a challenging timeframe."**

AVOID: "He disturbed me so many times, calling like that and hanging up without leaving a message. What's wrong with him?"

BETTER: **"As annoying as that was to have all those calls waking me up, I realize that he thought I wasn't there when he got my answering machine each time he called and he became really worried about me."**

Speak Easy Rules

Review and Summary:

6 | Every Style Can Be Successful

✓ Appreciate what distinguishes you from other people.

✓ Believe there are many good approaches to all situations.

✓ Leverage your preferred style.

✓ See value in expanding your communication repertoire.

✓ Broaden your horizons to include wider views.

7 | Armor For Abuse

The greatest cause for feeling hurt is the power you give to others. Feelings occur instantaneously without conscious awareness of the mechanisms that give birth to them. As spontaneous as our feelings are and as unaware as we usually are about their origins, there's always a root that underlies how we feel. Once you recognize that you're empowering someone else when you're hurt by their words and you are, on some level, *choosing* that particular feeling rather than simply feeling it, you can begin to empower yourself instead of the other person and take control of your emotions and the way you're communicating.

AVOIDING THE HOOK

Just as we have been looking at the differences that occur when we change how we communicate, we can also create a new way of listening so we can avoid being trapped by what others say to us.

✓ What would happen if you could listen without being vulnerable?

✓ What would happen if you could take in what a person is saying without becoming a part of what the person is saying?

✓ What would happen if you could respect another's view without feeling personally diminished – even when the negative view is about you?

It's up to each of us to recognize the bait. It's up to each of us to avoid taking the hook. Rather than be unsuspecting or naïve, we can be aware and recognize what's directly in front of us.

You Are Absolutely Right

A key device in the martial arts is to turn the strength of the attack back onto the attacker, without using your own force or aggression. You can easily neutralize a verbal attack in a similar way by reinforcing and capitalizing on a component of what someone has just said to you, without being defensive or indignant – and without compromising your own self-worth or belief system.

The simplest way to do this is to express that you recognize what a person is saying, without apologizing or defending.

ILLUSTRATION:
Realizing the temperature had finally risen to 63° outside, Nancy decided

to take a long walk at lunchtime on the first warm day in many weeks. After a brutally icy winter she couldn't bring herself to rush back to the office for the start of the weekly managers' meeting. She was not the last person to arrive at the meeting; at least three other managers followed her into the conference room, the last appeared ten minutes after her arrival.

It was jolting to see the CEO (Chief Executive Officer) from the company's corporate offices, located two hundred miles away, sitting in on the meeting that day. Nancy was surprised that no one had alerted people to the fact that the CEO would be attending the meeting. She definitely would have arrived on time, out of respect for the CEO, rather than linger coatless in the brilliantly warm early spring sunshine.

When the meeting was over, Nancy was singled out and accosted by the Managing Director of the firm who yelled at her in the middle of the open hallway just outside the conference room, in full earshot of many people, including clients and staff.

"You're always late to meetings. It was so disrespectful of you to come to the meeting late. How do you think it looked to Anne (CEO)? I hate it that you're always late."

Nancy silently counted to three (one one-thousand, two one-thousand, three one-thousand), taking some deep quiet breaths, and then calmly and simply replied with strength, neutral facial expression and good eye contact, *"You're absolutely right, Blair, it's really important to be on time."*

Since Blair was the one who had failed to let people know that Anne was attending the meeting, since numerous managers always arrived late to that meeting without explanation because of a variety of client calls or meetings that took precedence, since the meetings were always rather casual and loose, Nancy was, of course, baffled at Blair's strong, demeaning reaction and in particular at how Nancy seemed to be the only one catching flack publicly for her late arrival.

Instead of *taking the hook* and showing how angry she was, Nancy chose to take the high road and acknowledge an important fact that reflected what Blair had said to her and yet, in no way acknowledged any guilt, apology, responsibility for, or partici-

this whole book seems to be geared towards learning how to deal w/ abusive managers can we have a sequel that talks about dealing with the cause & not the symptoms?

118

pation in the damaging public accusation that she'd just received.

Our emotions and reactions often come between us and
the ideal communication paths. To the extent that you can
take several deep (and inaudible) breaths, stay calm and
detached, and make clear statements of fact, you will be
able to find responses that are comfortable to say in difficult challenging situations. Acknowledging that an important fact is correct is different from saying an accusation is
correct and is also quite different from taking on blame for
or defending that accusation.

Even when others are communicating to us in inappropriate ways, it's often better to take the high road like Nancy
than to enter the fray. This cost-benefit analysis is difficult to
see in the midst of an emotional response to abusive communication. The more you can remember to acknowledge
factual content rather than defend an emotional position,
the more easily it will be for you to manage your emotions
and avoid escalating communications that are damaging
and non-productive.

SILENCE IS GOLDEN
In our communications we often dig ourselves a hole and
then can't get out of it. Frequently, we feel it's necessary to
respond, defend, disclaim, explain, or even, attack when
silence would be the ideal choice.

Sometimes it's best to say nothing at all. Acknowledging through facial expression, eye contact and head nodding may be the ideal communication in many situations. You can convey that you're listening, you're sincere and you're giving attention, without saying a word.

 **REMINDER:**

> *It's critical to remember that a look of annoyance or frustration will convey more than words; if silence is the desired communication, your face must be silent as well.*

The less comfortable you are with silence, the more likely it will be that you will rush in to participate when non-participation would be the best choice possible. This is a silence of self-benefit, different from acquiescence or tail-between-the-legs silence. This is a silence of active listening and attentive acknowledgement.

WHEN THANK YOU IS ALL THAT IS NEEDED
A similar way of managing difficult or challenging communication is to respond with a thank you:

> *"Thank you for telling me this; it's important for me to know just how you are experiencing this situation."*

By thanking someone, you
- ✓ Indicate that you welcome openness
- ✓ Show that you want to increase your awareness
- ✓ Demonstrate that you value others' viewpoints

When we choose to respond like this, it's best to refrain from adding a disclaimer. If we say thank you to someone and then add, "**But** that isn't the way I see it.", we have erased the thank you and defeated its purpose. It's wonderful to expand on the positive and share differing perspectives. If the purpose of the "thank you" is to acknowledge without engaging in a debate or doing battle with someone, then END your communication at the *thank you*, rather than expand it.

Setting the stage for open communication is valuable in every setting. In addition to the benefit we gain from encouraging others to be open with us, this type of response – expressing appreciation for hearing what others think, see and feel – increases our ability to protect ourselves from exposing our own vulnerability and our emotions that are better kept private.

There's the unlikely potential that you will open an immediate floodgate with your *thank you* and the person you thank will take that opportunity to heave every thought and feeling possible on you. If that were to happen, it's an indication that the individual may have been withholding from you to the point of bursting or that you may have been giving signals that you don't welcome openness. Frequently, I hear individuals expressing how afraid they are to communicate what they want to say. Paradoxically, the very people they're afraid of often express how much they want others to be unafraid of being open with them. There really is very little down-side to saying thank you.

REMINDER:

> **Watch your tone. If your thank you has an exaggerated singsong sarcastic "Well, e-x-c-u-s-e me!" tone to it, the purpose will be defeated.**

An additional type of response to add to the mix, if the dialogue continues for too long or goes down an unexpected path, would be:

> *"This is valuable that you're telling me how you think and feel. Let's find another time that works for both of us to have a longer important conversation about all of this."*

EMBRACING THE CHILD INSIDE

In the examination of how words wound and produce hurtful emotions, it's critical to look at how our own internal words to ourselves are often the most destructive of all. We're usually our severest critics and worst enemies. We spend so much time focusing on and describing what others say to upset us that we're often blind to the self-inflicted verbal mistreatment we give to and receive from ourselves:

- "That was so stupid of me."
- "I'm so lazy."
- "I really messed that up."
- "I never seem to get it right."
- "I should have done this differently."
- "I should have known better."

- "What's wrong with me?"
- "Why didn't I remember to do that?"
- "Why can't I get anything right?"

We learn how destructive it is to talk to others in this way and set a goal to refrain from speaking to people so harshly, yet we admonish ourselves without giving any thought to validating our good side and reinforcing our own attributes.

When we experience extreme emotional reactions to what people are saying to us, there's usually something from our personal history that is stimulating those emotions. Whenever our feelings are out of proportion to an actual situation and we feel that our feelings and responses are out of control, there's often an underlying link to our past.

This kind of self-admonition and strong negative emotional response reflects a disconnection from our life history and a rejection of the child from our past who lives inside each of us. It's certainly better to focus on and be in the present than to live in and dwell on the past, yet if we never come to terms with, understand, and embrace the child who lives inside each of us, then it will remain difficult to live fully in the present and our emotions will control us rather than our being able to control our emotions.

As foreign as the concept of *the child within* may seem to you or as much as it sounds to you like touchy-feely psychobabble, it's a predominant communication obstacle that many people face and you may be one of them. Without recognition, self-acceptance and true self-affection, the child within will continue to dominate your feelings and control how you see the world, how you react to it and how you communicate.

The time and work it takes to arrive at a new place of self-acceptance requires dedication and often the benefit of professional support. There's certainly an abundance of literature that focuses in depth on these elements connected to the inner child. Rather than cite them or go into great detail on this important topic that greatly influences communication, here are some brief guidelines to begin to incorporate a new understanding of and a gentler approach to the child within:

- Examine the situations when you have exaggerated feelings or emotions/communications that are out of control.

- Look back at these situations to see if you can find the reprimanding judgmental self-talk that's going on in your head.

- Establish as best as you can at what age in your childhood or youth you think these reprimands most typically stem from.

- Think of the loving age-appropriate ways you can be self-accepting and loving towards that child.

- Develop a set of embracing new language to express to your child within.

- Find warmth and humor to engage the child rather than impatience and rejection.

- Be self-loving.

Since this concept can seem strange and artificial to people, I approach this topic cautiously with clients. It's a topic that may be unwelcome in the business world; it's not one that everyone needs to address; it's a subject that only certain people will want to look at. With sensitivity to the setting and the individual, when I see people dealing with repeating life-obstacles, I selectively examine with them what connection there is between the reoccurring obstacles and the child within.

Let's take a look at a scenario to see how this can work:

Hank's Temper

Hank had spent a lifetime getting into extreme arguments with people. He often felt his anger rising and was concerned that one day he would physically harm someone because of the extreme feelings he had when people criticized him or showed him what he saw as disrespect.

When Hank was a teenager, his father lost his job and spent hours at home every day for the first time since Hank was a baby. Because Hank's father had traveled so much for business, Hank and his mother had developed a wonderful closeness. Now that the father was no longer away all the time, the father began to do many of the chores and repairs in the house that Hank had taken over.

Since the father had lost his role at work and felt replaced in the home by Hank, the father began to tell Hank constantly what an inadequate and botched job Hank was doing.

Without realizing the connection, Hank grew into a man who repeated all of those criticisms to himself constantly. It took a bit of self-examination to realize where his anger was coming from and while he began to control the way he argued with others, he found no way to stop the harsh self-directed inner voice.

One morning, while shaving, Hank began to review the struggle he was having accepting the end of a relationship with a woman he'd been involved with for over three years and accepting that for the first time in his life he'd been going to see a counselor to look at his repeating patterns that always seemed to bring him to the end of relationships. As he went through the list of self-recriminations and self-judgments, he could feel himself getting angrier and angrier at himself as he spoke into the mirror:

"You should've been able to fix everything so that she wouldn't have left you. You should've been able to do it better. You're a loser who can't do anything right."

When Hank cut himself while shaving that morning, something clicked in his head, and he changed the self-talk into:

"I get how lousy you feel that she left you; you did everything you knew how to do to please her. You gave your all to this relationship and I love you for all the passion you brought to it. You're a great guy that gives one hundred percent and I know how hurt and disappointed you are that this didn't work out."

And then with a loving smile and a genuine wink, he said firmly and gently into the mirror,

"Hank, you just can't let your temper rule you anymore because you're going to send everybody you love away from you if you keep doing that. I won't let you do that anymore."

With an eeriness that Hank could not explain, he heard and saw the teen-aged Hank looking back at him from the mirror saying, "Hey, thanks, man! What took you so long to stop me? This anger gig has really been way too exhausting!"

What took so long was that for the first time Hank was able to feel self-loving. What was different this time was that Hank no longer was berating the teenaged Hank for being such a jerk. What truly distinguished this moment of truth from all previous attempts to make peace with himself was that Hank had stopped pushing away and abandoning the child within; this time there was an embrace. And for the first time, Hank was looking forward to his counseling session that evening. Maybe there was hope after all.

PUTTING AWAY THOSE MEASURING STICKS

Another element I frequently observe is the tendency people have to use a comparative measuring stick to feel defeated and to berate themselves. Reality checks are a good thing and knowing what is required to accomplish a goal is critical for success. If you bake a cake and put whimsical amounts of various ingredients into the mix because it's what you have on hand or what feels right in the moment, the likelihood of the cake being delicious is slim.

When you use measuring sticks to compare yourself to others and come up short, you can begin to feel hopeless and your communication can take a downward turn. It's much better to use the success of others for inspiration and motivation rather than for self-judgment and recrimination.

AVOID: "She's so much smarter than I am."
BETTER: **"She's such a wonderful inspiration."**

AVOID: "When I read a book that is fabulously written, I know I can never be a writer."
BETTER: **"When I read a book that is fabulously written, I am so lifted by the writing that I want to raise the level of my writing as high as possible."**

AVOID: "When I went to my high school reunion, I felt so unaccomplished. All of my buddies are Vice Presidents and making huge incomes."
BETTER: **"When I went to my high school reunion and saw the level of achievement and earning power of my old friends, I decided to look deeply at the satisfaction and pride I get from my work as a drug counselor and that old desire I have to enter the business arena and make big bucks."**

I often suggest to my clients that they buy a measuring device, a ruler, a tape measure, a calculator or even a metronome for those who appreciate music. I tell them to pick out a beautiful or fine object they can keep in a prominent place as a reminder to turn measurement into inspiration. I also suggest that if they have an important presentation or an interview or conversation on their calendar that's quite important to them, that they place that measuring device in a box, a drawer, a closet or a container to symbolize how important it is to be respectful of measurements and how important it is not to be taking those self-defeating ways of measuring themselves or communicating to their meetings and presentations.

CHOOSING EXCELLENCE OVER PERFECTION

The toughest measurement of all is *PERFECTION*. Many people set that unattainable standard for themselves, which inevitably leads to disappointment. When perfection is the objective, then nothing less than 100% will satisfy and even 99.99% will signify failure. If *EXCELLENCE* is the goal instead, it will always be attainable. Pride and satisfaction can be achieved through the quest for excellence and there will constantly be new ways to raise the bar for enhancement. Whenever you are getting ready to say "Perfect!", choose "Excellent!" instead.

The human side of communication is multi-layered and complex. The more we understand all of these layers and the more self-aware we become, the stronger we will feel and the more enhanced our communication will be.

Speak Easy Rules

Review and Summary:

7 | Armor For Abuse

✓ Dissolve people's power to hurt you with their words.

✓ Recognize when silence would be the best response.

✓ Thank people, without defensiveness, for being open.

✓ Take care of your internal emotional trigger points.

✓ Refrain from measuring yourself harshly against others.

Speak Easy:
The Situations

8 | Refusing The Right Way

We began our voyage with a wide array of basic guidelines to prepare us for a smooth communication ride. Next, we traveled inwardly to examine the many ways our individual personal styles, perspectives, and experiences influence the way we see the world and communicate. Now we're ready to take excursions into various specific situations to put into practice what we've learned and to gain focused communication skills for each of them. Let's start with a common situation where most people report feeling discomfort and difficulty.

It's rare to find a person who is completely comfortable saying no. For some reason the legitimacy of the refusal is often overshadowed by guilt, embarrassment, intimidation or lack of a sense of legitimacy. As a result of these uncomfortable feelings, people have a tendency to say yes when they want to say no; to explain, defend and apologize when unnecessary; and to agree to unwanted conditions or qualify their refusals in ways that are out of sync with their actual intentions and desires.

Learning how to refuse a request completely, appropriately and comfortably is an essential element of being a good communicator. If you acquire the ability to refuse requests respectfully and completely without conditions and without apologies, you will be able to discern and decide:

✓ When to say yes
✓ When to agree partially or conditionally
✓ When to apologize legitimately for refusing
✓ When to refuse 100%

Always Keep It Level

No matter how outrageous or reasonable someone's request is, you can acknowledge and respect the person's right to make the request without judgment or obligation. The first step in refusing a request appropriately is to remember the level playing field of equal two-way communication:

By focusing on the principle of equal and level communication, you can avoid expressing inappropriate feelings like intimidation, condescension or guilt. No matter how you view the request, it's important for your tone, facial expression, and word choice to reflect mutual respect and communication equality. Even when you're asserting authority, laying down the law, or simply expressing clarity of viewpoint, the tone and content of the communication can be calm and mutually respectful.

Focus On The Other Person

You can always recognize a person's viewpoint sympathetically, respectfully, objectively and politely, without participation or apology.

Validation

VALIDATION EXAMPLES:

- "I hear how much you want to go out to dinner."
- "It's so clear how important it is to you that I participate in this event."
- "I can see that your heart is set on doing this."
- "I recognize that your foremost goal is to gain corporate approval."

It's natural to have personal reactions with negative overtones to what others ask of us: being insulted, feeling superior, thinking the request is stupid, having an extremely different point of view, sensing that someone is using you, wanting to defend against or attack the person making the request, etc. When these types of reactions get in the way of responding respectfully, the focus gets lost, the person making the request has equally strong opposing reactions that follow, and an escalation of feelings and reactions color the communication, leading to confrontation and/or leaving a bad taste on both sides. The more you can listen without judgment, demonstrate that you've heard, and focus on validating the legitimacy of the request, the easier it will be to set a neutral and comfortable tone for refusal and for level communication.

SAY WHAT YOU WANT, MEAN WHAT YOU SAY
Making the actual and clear refusal is the biggest challenge for people. Often the response sounds so drawn out, convoluted, and explanatory that the refusal isn't actually heard and the door is left wide open. This sets the stage for the person making the request to jump right back in and push the agenda further or find ways to adjust the request and corner the person who just refused in a poor or ambiguous manner.

Refusing simply for the sake of refusing is far from optimum and asserting your refusal just because you've learned how to refuse "correctly" is also an empty strategy. As strange as it may seem, I've often observed people refusing in either of these arbitrary ways. Since refusing is so difficult for so many, once someone learns how to refuse, there can be a tendency to refuse automatically to show off the new ability or to avoid slipping back into being seen as Mr. or Ms. Pushover. The refusal must be the desired and real response to the actual request and must match the true wishes of the respondent. Make sure that when you've decided you want to refuse, you do it strongly, appropriately and clearly. And remember to begin with a specific and genuine validation of the person making the request to show how well you've listened and to demonstrate that you've understood what's important to that person even though you're refusing the request. Here are some guiding examples that demonstrate how to refuse requests:

Friend responding to a request to go out to dinner

"I hear how much you want to go out to dinner tonight. I can't possibly go with you because of all the work I've committed to finish before tomorrow's meeting. Thanks for asking me. I hope you have a great evening."

Colleague responding to a request to participate in an event at work

"It's so clear how much you'd like me to participate in this event. As important as it is to you and as much as I recognize the value of what you're doing, I'm certain that I don't want to be a participant. Even though I'm refusing your request, I thank you for asking me and know you will be successful without me."

Friend responding to a request to sponsor and endorse a community project

"I can see that your heart and mind are set on making this happen. I know you've been totally focused on this project for the last six months. As respectful as I am of the work you've done, I can't endorse or participate in your campaign because I see the goals quite differently. I would appreciate it very much if you didn't ask me again to join your efforts or donate to your cause."

Boss/Manager responding to a request for approval

"I recognize how much you want to gain corporate approval for your plan. I see how well you've mapped out the agenda and benefits. I won't be able to participate in any way to move you closer to gaining this approval. It was appropriate that you came to me and I appreciate knowing what your approach is. I can't give you my approval or participation."

Friend/Family Member responding to a request to loan money

"I see what a challenging timeframe this is for you and I know how hard it was to ask me to loan you the money you need. Because of a painful experience of loaning money to someone I loved very much, I promised myself a long time ago that I'd never loan money again to anyone no matter who it was or what the circumstances were. It's painful to refuse what you're asking me because I care about you so much even though I'm completely committed to standing by that promise I've lived by for so many years. I'm always here for you to listen and support you in any other way that I can."

There are key reasons for making these responses as harsh as they may seem to certain readers. Rather than look at them as harsh, it's better to see how _clear_, _direct_ and _respectful_ they are. While demonstrating clarity, they also represent the extreme case of _100%_ refusal. Depending on the situation, there could be numerous appropriate ways of responding to these same requests, from saying yes, to partial agreement with multiple conditions. Since this section of the book began with an acknowledgment of how difficult it is for many people to refuse requests, _all of these examples communicate total refusals_.

> **It's important to reiterate that if you can learn to refuse a request completely in a mutually respectful manner, you will then be able to refuse or grant requests totally or partially in a variety of ways that fit your goals and those of others.**

There are actually two layers of skill involved in refusing requests. _The emphasis here is on the communication_, on being able to find the right way to respond in refusing a request. The underlying and quite important second skill is assessing and recognizing what the right response is given the particulars involved. _Knowing when to refuse and when not to refuse is a critical assessment to make._

> *In every situation, including those where refusing a request can have great risk or severe downside, there is always an optimum way to communicate a refusal.*

It's valuable to be a *can-do* person who likes to *make-it-happen* when people come to you. It's good to see how you can be someone who delivers and thinks about pleasing others and meeting their needs. Certainly, there are circumstances when you're obligated, or it's wise, to say yes to requests that are the opposite of your true wishes. In many of these situations, refusing a request is an unwise and undesirable choice. In the vast majority of circumstances, there are ways to refuse appropriately and respectfully, when the decision to refuse is the right one. The more comfortable you can become in gaining the skill of refusing requests, the more easily you will face challenging requests well and effectively. You will greatly enhance how you handle difficult requests, by knowing what you want your response to be, developing the communication skills to deliver your refusals well, and using the three key approaches just outlined:

1. KEEP IT LEVEL
2. FOCUS ON AND VALIDATE THE OTHER PERSON
3. SAY WHAT YOU WANT, MEAN WHAT YOU SAY

REMINDER:

> *When you adapt your communications, even when there is desired improvement, people often respond with surprise or discomfort. If you typically say yes, you may hear unexpected reactions to legitimate refusals. People's negativity may be coming from expectations based on your prior patterns of responding. Also, with your new ways of responding, you may unknowingly contribute further to negative reactions because you're exaggerating or concentrating on your new approaches, causing you to sound insincere, canned, or extreme.*

As people set out to refuse requests, using the simple guides mapped out in this chapter, they often miss the mark. They think they are:

- Communicating well in a level tone (1)
- Listening carefully and validating the person making the request (2)
- Expressing a clear refusal with no open doors (3)

Instead, they often have a tone that's far from level, have forgotten or missed providing real validation, and have been too heavy-handed, ambiguous, or unclear.

ADVICE:

✓ Get feedback from a coach or peer group so you will understand how well your delivery matches your intentions.

✓ Rehearse and test out using these communications in a safe "practice" environment before relying on them in challenging circumstances.

Speak Easy Rules

Review and Summary:

8 | Refusing The Right Way

✓ Remain at ease when people make difficult requests.

✓ Validate people's right to ask for what they want.

✓ Match your responses with what you can really deliver.

✓ Be clear when your intention is to refuse completely.

✓ Think through your response before you say yes.

9 | Expanding Your "Who You Know" Quotient

Let's continue our communication journey, examining another life situation that applies to everyone and requires comfortable smooth communication, above all, for success. In this chapter, we will see how good communication is the key to accomplished networking.

Many people think of networking as a primary job search tool. As much as that's true, it would be foolish to see it in such a limited way. Networking is much more than a critical job search ingredient; it's one of the key factors that contribute to good career development and successful career management. Moreover, it's a primary and essential *life tool* at every level and in every facet of human activity and human endeavor. The exact same networking concepts can be applied in limitless life arenas from recruiting, sales, fundraising, and taskforce development to the pursuit of a life partner or the search for a good electrician or a new school for your children. It's extremely rare that any person can exist and thrive without networking. The more you enhance your communication skills, the more you will succeed in networking and the more comfortable you will become doing it.

How often have you heard statements similar to these?

- "It's not *what* you know, it's *who* you know."
- "Networking is the key to finding a new ___ (job, spouse, plumber, etc.)."
- "He made it to the top because he's part of the *Old Boys'* network."
- "She didn't make it because she was so busy with her

nose to the grindstone that she never paid attention to making connections with the right people."

We will encounter much more success in all of our endeavors when we recognize the high value of gathering information from real people who've traveled the road before us and of building strong and lasting bonds with them.

There is great variety in individual styles and comfort levels when it comes to engaging new people and nourishing relationships with those outside of an already well known or familiar circle. In Chapter Six, we looked at the opposite approaches of being an *Initiator* or a *Responder*. These two preferences play an important role in a person's desire, approach and ease with the valuable activity, most often referred to as networking. A review of that section of Chapter Six will contribute to your being more self-aware and in tune with your most comfortable ways to bring skilled networking communications into the forefront of your life.

The word, NETWORKING, is used so freely and widely that its basic meaning has been diluted and it has lost many of its most important nuances and benefits. When career advisors emphasize the importance of networking, they often neglect to teach its subtleties adequately and to fine-tune their clients' networking communications well. It's easy to see why many jobseekers think that networking is simply informing as many people as possible that they're looking for a new job.

Certainly, letting people know you're looking for a new job is a much better strategy than simply sitting by the phone, waiting to see if someone will call you up to offer you a job. However, if your bottom line is no more than a numbers approach of seeing how many people you can get your resume in front of, the benefits of the fine art of networking will be sadly missed and the process of continuing the endeavor will become stale and unrewarding. After all, how many times can you say to someone, "Here I am again, still looking. Got anything for me?" No wonder people become so disenchanted with networking – both on the asking AND on the receiving end!

Since the term, NETWORKING, is so freely used and so often badly leveraged, I'd like to refer to it in other terms going forward. My definition of this word appeared a few paragraphs back:

> **The high value of gathering information from real people who have traveled the road before us and of building strong and lasting bonds with them**

To alleviate its limited and stereotypical definition, I'm going to rename NETWORKING as **R&R: Research and Relationships.** The "N" word translates into the **R&R** formula:

Research and Relationships

=

Gathering Information/Building Connections

It's also fun and gratifying to refer to an activity like NETWORKING that people find difficult, tiring and demanding as **R&R**, a known acronym for Rest and Relaxation. How delightful to re-label NETWORKING communications with a symbol of pleasure and satisfaction that people always seek out and appreciate! **RESEARCH AND RELATIONSHIPS** are the anchors for this chapter.

THE NEW APPROACH: PASSION FIRST

Whenever people are energized by the subjects they're talking about, others are drawn toward these speakers. Without passion for a topic, even if it's your unanswered quest to find a new job, you will find little enthusiasm from others around you. The trick is to find the elements that you can remain passionate about and make sure they're at the forefront of your **R&R** communications.

It's critical to initiate **R&R** communications with enthusiasm:

> ✓ "What I most want to talk to people about is customer service. I find it endlessly exciting (interesting, engaging, gratifying, wonderful, etc.) to share ideas about how people are using technology today to accomplish (rebuild, develop, create, demonstrate, etc.) client services programs."

An unappealing image that often blocks people's natural agility in and genuine enthusiasm for networking communications is the hat-in-hand beggar needing a handout.

"Please can you feed me?"
"Please can you help me find a job?"
"Please fix my problem."

This empty-plate approach to networking is what gives people such an uneasy feeling about it and what takes them so far away from the main concepts of **R&R: RESEARCH AND RELATIONSHIPS.**

Finding ways to engage others in conversation about your key interests and to demonstrate how knowledgeable you are ensures a much better approach to people and a much higher success rate in obtaining meetings with others. There's also the added benefit of feeling strong and focused when you're sitting down with someone to have an important **R&R** conversation.

BE THE ONE WITH THE IDEAS
So often, people begin a request for a networking meeting with, "I'd just like to pick your brain." This clichéd phrase inserts a terrible graphic picture into the process and contributes, on both sides of the communication, to the concept of begging or neediness. Picking a brain is what vultures do to dead animal carcasses. Picking a brain is a one-sided approach to a conversation and demonstrates taking from someone rather than contributing to a dialogue. In contrast, if the request for an R&R meeting is to brainstorm

ideas together, the stage and tone will be set for an entirely different communication. Brainstorming is a two-sided (or multi-sided) approach to a conversation and demonstrates bringing something to the table to engage in a give-and-take dialogue.

× **Brain-picking**   ✓ **Brainstorming**

Another overused phrasing often applied in networking communication is, "Jane Doe recommended that I contact you." or "John Doe referred me to you." In addition to being the same ol', same ol' that everyone else is saying, these worn-out introductions are stated in the undesirable passive voice. In Chapter 4, the first tool we looked at in the Speak Easy Toolbox was the elimination of the passive voice. Beyond being trite and passive, this style of communication misses an important opportunity to demonstrate initiative and ownership. Here's a much better way of presenting yourself to someone while still introducing the key element of an important contact's name and influence:

> ✓ "Yesterday I had a great conversation with Jane Doe. I told Jane how interested I am in speaking to people about Human Resources compensation planning and Jane and I agreed that you would be a wonderful person for me to meet."

Flattery Gets You Everywhere, You Just Have To Mean It

An even better enhancement to add to this type of new and improved, direct, proactive, individualized, self-introduction is:

> ✓ "Yesterday I had a great conversation with Jane Doe. I told Jane how interested I am in speaking to people about Human Resources compensation programs and Jane told me about the wonderful work you've done at JKL Company in this area. She and I agreed that you'd be a terrific person for me to meet. I'm particularly interested in talking to you and comparing notes on how you managed the transition from the QRS system to the ABC system at JKL. What an amazing accomplishment to have completed in that short a timeframe with such a limited resource base."

When you can express genuine appreciation and admiration for an individual, you will be adding another important layer to your **R&R** communication. It's critical that:

> ✓ You know specific elements about a person's experience to underscore and praise the person for.
> ✓ Your praise is genuine.
> ✓ Your tone and content are authentic.

Nothing can be less appealing than a plastic complement that's saccharin and insincere. Nothing can be more appealing than praise that expresses genuine appreciation.

Face To Face Is Best

People are frequently hesitant to ask busy and important individuals for meetings. Most often this hesitance is from:

> ✗ Lack of self-confidence: "No one wants to meet with me."

- ✗ Distress from meeting new people: "I'm uncomfortable asking to meet you."
- ✗ Desire for expedience: "I want the most from you in the least time."
- ✗ Respect for time constraints: "I respect how demanding your life is."

Here are two contrasting illustrations that will challenge these paths of thought and motivate you to recognize the value of getting face-to-face meetings with people versus limiting your communications to the phone or to email.

PHONE CONVERSATION WITH PERSON A:
"Hello, my name is Rachel Lehcar and my roommate, Sarah Haras, was in the workshop you did for Big Bad Company last week. ✓
She told me that you were the best facilitator she's ever had in a workshop and I wanted to thank you for reenergizing her. ✓ *She was starting to be very depressed but since your workshop she's returned to her wonderful highly motivated self.* ✓

I do the same kind of work you do and the firm I work for is closing all of its east coast offices next month; Sarah told me how jammed your schedule is so I'd like to just ask you for the name of the Managing Director of your office who does the hiring of new trainers. ✗ *I'd like to contact that person to see if there is any work available for someone like me.*× *May I please use your name when I introduce myself to your Managing Director?"*×

PHONE CONVERSATION WITH PERSON B:
"Hi. My name is Clara Aralc and I got your name from a mutual friend that we share, Tom Mott.✓ **Tom told me what a terrific workshop facilitator you are and how much we have in common.**✓ **In addition to doing the same type of work that you do, I'm a dog enthusiast. Tom told me how much you love dogs.**✓

Since the firm I work for is closing all of its east coast offices next month, I have decided that I would like to meet the best facilitators in our industry to compare notes and gain a strong handle on what the best training practices are on the market today.✓ **I want to get an inside view of the lay of the land of the top training firms out there so I can decide what environments are right for me and so I can present myself as strongly as possible.**✓

From how Tom described you, you're just the kind of person I'd like to talk to.✓ **When's a good time for us to meet?**✓ **What works**

> *best for you?*✓ *My schedule is*
> *flexible and I can meet you right*
> *before work or right after or at*
> *lunchtime.*✓ *It would be fun to*
> *grab some lunch together if that's*
> *a comfortable thing to do.*✓ *John*
> *tells me how nice you are and how*
> *alike he thinks we are."*✓

Rachel, Person A, starts out terrifically. She has an actual contact that she names and her comments are quite individualized and flattering. Yet she rapidly goes downhill in this introductory conversation. Because she's respectful of limited time availability, she destroys her great beginning by asking right away for the name of the person who is in charge of hiring. There are serious negative repercussions for moving so quickly and asking such direct questions rather than asking for a meeting.

First of all, she's asking to compete for work with the person she's speaking to. In essence, she's saying, "I'd like to ask your boss for a job like yours (or even for your job)." Secondly, even though she has introduced herself through a known contact which is always better than a cold call, she's asking for an introduction to someone's manager when she's actually, at the point in time of the conversation, a total stranger. Very few people would be comfortable making an introduction of their boss to someone they've never met in person.

Thirdly, by going immediately for the name of the person in charge of hiring rather than asking for a meeting to establish a relationship and gain a broad base of information, Rachel has actually brought the conversation to its end, cutting off the valuable **R&R** benefit she may have gained if she'd gone slower and focused on having a dialogue rather than winning the prize. And lastly, she has set the stage for the person hearing her questions to hang up the phone and go straight to the Managing Director's office and say, "If someone by the name of Rachel Lehcar contacts you looking for work and uses my name, I want you to know that she's a total stranger who called me today and I don't know anything about who she is and didn't give her permission to use my name to contact you."

Person B, Clara Aralc, sets the tone for a wonderful first meeting. She has just the right balance of friendliness and professionalism. She's clear about wanting to have a meeting to exchange information and build a connection. She sets the stage to gain introductions to referrals by first becoming a known entity and demonstrating who she is. She's respectful and confident. After the subsequent meeting that will take place as a result of this phone conversation, Clara will have established herself as a person to be introduced to the Managing Director, to be referred to others and as a person who will be welcomed as a contact in the future.

If a primary goal is to expand your current network of contacts and to build new relationships with key individuals, then meeting in person is a paramount objective.

Turn Off The Pressure
When you come to the table expecting or needing a handout, you're coming from an unequal and undesirable position. When you expect another person to fix your problem or feed you, you're creating internal pressure for yourself and pressure that repels that person away from you; you're increasing the likelihood of disappointment and dead-end.

There are many people who naturally like to help and tapping into that appropriately and sensitively is good. Recognizing and defining your goals and then coming to the right resources to supply you with what you're seeking can be managed from a position of strength rather than weakness and can attract people to you rather than turn them away from you.

The keys are to:

- ✓ Find a way to turn off the pressure for yourself and for the person you are approaching.
- ✓ Define and communicate what you want in ways that can be easily satisfied.
- ✓ Establish a genuine connection that you can return to over time

You will have done the lion's share of what you need to do to remove pressure from your **R&R** communications if you start with your focus on a topic you're passionate about, remove passive language from your introduction and identify ways to express praise and admiration.

Here are two basic ways to approach people for **R&R** that will greatly reduce the pressure that's felt on both sides of networking communications:

- ✓ **"I'm gathering information from knowledgeable people that I respect highly so I can make solid decisions about how I want to move forward."**

- ✓ **"I'm talking to key people who have their fingers on the pulse of the marketplace so I can be as well informed, up-to-date and as professionally competitive as possible."**

REMOVE THE POSSIBILITY OF YES AND NO
IT'S ALL ABOUT THE QUESTIONS

One of the most useful **R&R** communication skills you can develop is to ask questions artfully, questions that demonstrate how well prepared you are and that contribute to establishing a strong relationship going forward. You want to make a mark, set yourself apart from the crowd and leave a lasting impression.

What are the ingredients of an artful question? The most important one is to ask open-ended questions that give the respondent the most freedom to give an expansive answer in return. You will have the least likelihood of receiving thoughtful and full responses when you ask questions that can be answered with "YES" or "NO" so it's critical to avoid questions that begin with the following words:

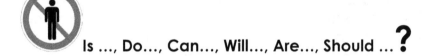

Is ..., Do..., Can..., Will..., Are..., Should ... **?**

Less effective: "Do you know anyone else I can speak to about this?"

More effective: "Who are others that you recommend I speak to?"

Less effective: "Can you tell me what other resources I should be using"

More effective: "What other resources are important for me to include?"

Less effective: "Will you be able to give me a solution to this problem?"

More effective: "What do you see as the best solutions to this situation?"

Less effective: *"Should I be approaching my goals in this way?"*

More effective: *"What are the best ways to approach these goals?"*

Less effective: *"Is there more you can tell me about this topic?"*

More effective: *"What else do you think is important for me to consider?"*

Delightful Devices – Let Us Count The Ways

Whenever you can approach someone with a legitimate request for information or a specific topic to discuss, you will achieve much more mileage if you bring something to the table when you make your request. You will gain the most in return by demonstrating that you see solutions and that you're in the process of making decisions. People will give you the least in return when they sense you want them to fill an empty plate, provide you with solutions, make choices for you, or repair your problems. So in addition to asking open-ended questions, it's important to bring information and solutions when you're asking for information, seeking advice or examining solutions.

Less effective: *"Do you know anyone else I can speak to about this?"*

More effective: *"Who are others that you recommend I speak to?"*

Most effective: *"Here is a brief list of the kind of people I'd like to speak to. Who are the people on this list that you know I can speak to? What other people does it make sense to add to this list? If you were making a list like this, who'd be on your list?"*

Less effective: *"Can you tell me what other resources I should be using?"*

More effective: *"What other resources are important for me to include?"*

<u>Most</u> **effective**: *"Here are the resources, the ways I have used them, and how I've found them to be useful as I make decisions about this situation. What do you think of these and of how I'm using them? What others do you recommend? What are some other ways to leverage these as I move forward?"*

Less effective: *"Is there more you can tell me about this topic?"*

More effective: *"What else do you think is important for me to consider about this topic?"*

<u>Most</u> **effective**: *"Here are some other considerations I'm looking at and the value I see in including them. How do you see these? What additional important perspective have I overlooked? What else comes to mind when you look at what I've described?"*

Another important component to add to these **R&R** conversations is customization. The individuals I coach often bring me their all-purpose, one-stop-shopping "networking scripts" for me to critique. While I certainly want to make life easy for people who are doing a lot of time-consuming work to prepare for networking meetings and definitely never recommend reinventing-the-wheel approaches, I also refuse to critique, or recommend using, communications that are going to be mechanically spewed out for every situation. Whenever you can tailor your communications in an individualized manner to a specific individual and particular situation, you will greatly enhance the depth of response you get in return and increase the inroads you will make toward demonstrating your assets and building genuine relationships with others.

Less effective: *"Will you be able to give me a solution to this problem?"*

More effective: *"What do you see as the best solutions to this situation?"*

<u>Most</u> effective: *"I see how successfully you accomplished XXX by using YYY. I see these parallels between your experience and what I'm considering. What other similarities are there? What have you learned from XXX that I could benefit from? What else.........."*

There are so many wonderful innovative ways to build a new network of contacts and to be able to communicate and interact with new people. Creating a survey, inviting people to participate in it, writing a report based on the information and data you collect, and getting that report in front of a larger audience combine beautifully to establish a wonderful platform to expand your "Who-You-Know" quotient and to provide multiple ways to communicate to others what's important.

PUT ON A SHOW – GIVE THEM FREE SAMPLES

It's advantageous to go beyond talking about what you do and what you're passionate about. Live demonstrations far outweigh limited descriptive conversations. Creating ways for people to see you performing in action will set you apart from others, leave a lasting impression, and strengthen relationships. There's also the full circle of benefit to be gained. Actions speak louder than words. And when you're in the live process of demonstrating or presenting something that you're familiar with and know well, your communications will be optimum as a result of the natural platform your activity or demonstration provides.

Providing free samples of your work can often be much more valuable than being paid a dollar amount for it or withholding your talent because there's no remuneration. Here are just a few of the ways you can work for free and demonstrate your excellent communication and professional skills to gain an advantage:

✓ Identify an association or group that you can make a presentation to on an important topic. Invite key people to listen to you present.

✓ Write an in-depth research report in your field of interest with professional analysis and recommendations. Send this report to key individuals and arrange for meetings with them to discuss your findings and recommendations.

✓ Ask to facilitate a workshop for a club, association or workgroup and make sure key individuals participate in it or observe it.

✓ Write an article on an important topic that you care about passionately and send it to people that matter to you. Get it published if possible.

Fine tuning your **R&R** communication approach in all of these superb, subtle and significant ways can generate dramatic changes in your perspective on and experience of networking. It can dramatically influence how people respond to you and, more importantly, how splendidly you can develop and demonstrate your communication skills.

 **REMINDER:**

> *Avoid asking questions that begin with "WHY" because they can be heard as accusatory. If you want to know why a person did something, ask instead:*
>
> *"Tell me how you decided to ... "*
> *or*
> *"What were the reasons you chose ... "*
>
> *"WHY" is the one open-ended question to eliminate from your repertoire.*

Speak Easy Rules

Review and Summary:

9 | Expanding Your "Who You Know" Quotient

✓ See NETWORKING as research and relationship building.

✓ Include solutions when discussing your challenges.

✓ Believe you have or can access the right contacts.

✓ Share what you know when you ask important questions.

✓ View NETWORKING as more than spreading your name.

10 | Working It At Work

After such a close look at networking communications, a natural next stop along our communication route is career management. This chapter is about managing your career strategically through effective communication. In Adele Scheele's *Skills for Success – Making the System Work for You,* she identifies the key characteristics that contribute to career success. One of those characteristics is defined by Scheele as the ability to "Risk Linking"; she describes this relationship-building trait as an essential ingredient for career achievement. *Expanding Your "Who You Know" Quotient,* the preceding *Speak Easy* chapter, focuses on this same critical life and career enhancing tool and serves as the primary foundation for this current chapter. Because of its major significance in career management and communication excellence, it's essential to incorporate *Expanding Your "Who You Know" Quotient* into the elements that follow here.

This chapter will concentrate primarily on the many and varied ways you can enhance your overall professional communications to pave the way for your advancement at work. Since many people become so uncomfortable and artificial on job interviews that they come across in mechanical and unnatural ways, this chapter will focus secondarily on the job interview. The elements of the following career management guidelines and seven-pronged approach to good career communication will also provide an excellent framework for job interview preparation.

With this focus in mind, you can start to realize that every day is an opportunity to demonstrate your level of accomplishment through your communication. By looking at communication in this way, you will be relaxed about, confident about, and prepared for any step along your career path whether you are up for a promotion, negotiating a salary increase, making a marketing presentation to a client, interviewing internally for a new position inside your company, meeting senior executives for the first time, or even actually out there on a job search.

VISUALIZE THE BRIDGE – CONNECTING IS EVERYTHING

Losing focus causes serious communication stumbles and poor speaking performance. Often people speak out freely and move from one topic to the next without purpose. Frequently they ramble excessively or get carried away talking about topics that interest them or that they think they're supposed to be addressing that have no connection to the individual on the receiving end of their communication. Sometimes they're simply nervous and can't think of what to say or how to say it.

One of the best devices to help you stay on topic and speak with relevance and confidence is to picture a bridge that connects you to the person you're talking to.

Bridging Connecting Linking

The image of the bridge can contribute to focus and relevance, can keep you in tune with and aware of the person you're speaking to, and can also be a reminder of the importance of the level two-way mutually respectful communication that this book repeatedly emphasizes.

Your ability to connect in a personal and genuine way with the other person in a two-way communication can be the single most important ingredient you bring to your communications and the single most important element the bridge symbolically represents. If you fail to connect with people when you speak to them, it's unlikely they will be listening to you or retaining what you're telling them and it's almost guaranteed that their primary objective will be to end the conversation with you as soon as possible. Somewhere in their minds they will be thinking, "NEXT": next coworker, next job candidate, next moment of privacy, next friend, next whatever; they just won't feel connected; they won't want to be with you.

There are many ways to connect with others. One of the primary ways is through eye contact. We saw that the *Responder* in Chapter Six prefers to break eye contact for reflection. I once coached a computer programmer who was so reflective when he was speaking that his eyes rolled all the way back behind his blinking eyelids in such a way that you could see only the whites of his eyes when he was talking. He was totally unaware of this behavior and had no idea of the negative impact this was having on the people he was communicating with. It was quite challenging for him to change this natural tendency and old habit and be able to connect with people through eye contact when speaking to them.

As important as credentials, experience, talent, expertise and technical skills are, without a personal and human connection to your coworkers and your work environment, there's little opportunity for career success. And it's extremely rare that a person will be hired for credentials and experience alone without also making a strong personal connection. It's important to bring the complete package to the bridge and to your communications.

Credentials Experience Expertise
Personality Chemistry Values

LIFE WITHOUT FEEDBACK

Getting accurate feedback is quite beneficial because none of us can see ourselves the way others see us. And in spite of their opposite definitions, perception *is* reality:

PERCEPTION = REALITY

Since our intentions often vary greatly from our actual impact on people, an extremely valuable contributor to our career success is establishing a method to receive honest, open feedback about our interactions and communications with others. To be able to recognize the influence of the ways we're relating and responding to people is one of the biggest communication challenges and can be one of the best career enhancers we can gain, if done in a way that's reassuring to feedback providers.

It's tremendously valuable to ask for and receive feedback from those around you from a wide variety of levels and roles. When you ask for feedback, you must assure others that you're genuinely open to receiving it: the good, the bad and the ugly. You must also pledge to people that their feedback matters to you and you want to incorporate what they're telling you into, not only a new self-awareness, but also into enhanced behaviors and communications.

If people see you as defensive, insecure, rigid, arrogant, vindictive or indifferent, they will find it hard to risk giving you open feedback. Even without these types of traits or being perceived as having them, it can be extremely difficult for people to be comfortable giving you honest feedback. Additionally, the higher up your role is in the hierarchy and on the food chain, the harder it becomes for people to have access to you and feel at ease saying what they really think or feel about you.

One way to resolve this dilemma is to engage the services of an external professional executive coach, skilled in collecting feedback so that that people are confident their:

✓ Anonymity will be protected.
✓ Confidentiality will be respected.
✓ Input will be well represented.
✓ Comfort with the process will be ensured.

These factors are not always well embodied in all feedback gathering practices. If the process lacks any of these ingredients, it can result in more damage than benefit.

360-degree feedback – feedback that comes from a full circle of individuals including superiors, peers, subordinates and others – is a highly valuable tool if certain parameters are met. The 360-degree feedback can be significantly meaningful if it's collected through personal interviews conducted by an independent consultant who can establish rapport, build trust easily and ensure confidentiality.

CAREER STRATEGIES 101 – THE 7-PRONGED APPROACH

When I'm advising people in preparation for a job interview or professional meeting, I always recommend the following simple seven-pronged approach. This communication arsenal equips individuals to be strong, confident and competitive in the job market. It is clear these approaches also provide a solid foundation for career success on the job. Think of these fundamentals as your **Career Gym Communication Workout** and know that a workday without exercising them is a day without career fitness.

YOUR CAREER GYM COMMUNICATION WORKOUT

1. **Be prepared.**
2. **Be positive.**
3. **Give "live" illustrations.**
4. **Avoid limiting qualifiers.**
5. **Be focused.**
6. **Avoid negative assumptions.**
7. **Be consistent.**

PRONG 1: NEVER BE EMPTY HANDED – ARRIVE FULLY LOADED
Groundwork plays a significant role in career advancement. A fundamental key to achieving professional success is being well-prepared:

PROFESSIONAL SUCCESS

 =

BEING WELL-PREPARED

It's critical to do your homework for any type of professional or work-related meeting that you're going to attend or participate in, no matter the size or the venue. It's often been said that:

"Information is Power!"

We live in *The Age of Information* and have immediate, easy, electronic access to an abundance of data we've never before had in the history of human existence. It's against your best interests to come into any professional dialogue without doing your homework or collecting data to support your views or position and to ensure you're well-informed and current. Doing the research to prepare for how you will communicate in a meeting sets you up for achievement and recognition.

PRONG 2 – PLAY UP THE POSITIVE

Whenever you determine that something won't work or isn't working, make sure you find a way to convey, "This is exactly what we need to do to make this successful." Rather than describe what's wrong, it's always better to focus on communicating the solutions to fix the situation.

In Chapter Four, the fourth tool in the Speak Easy Toolbox is *Say It Without the Not*. Even though we've already looked at this important component of language formation and human perspective, it's well worth revisiting and refocusing on this communication aspect in relation to career management and career advancement. When you challenge yourself to be a person that sees the world from a positive perspective and to focus on what *is* rather than on what *isn't*, you will find that you will gain respect from others and draw them to you. You will also be building a reputation as a person who finds ways to get things accomplished rather than as a person who tears everything down through doubt and criticism.

REMINDER:

> *Negativity can be quite subtle. Even the most positive sentiments can have a negative underbelly:*

- *"No problem!"* is a positive expression comprised of **two negative words.**

- Saying, *"I've no objection to..."* is very different from saying, *"I think that's a good way to..."*

- Stating, *"I can't disagree with you about..."* has quite a different impact from saying, *"I certainly agree with you that..."*

If you're in the middle of a conversation or a job interview and someone asks you for the worst example you can give on a subject, take the high road that represents you well in how you answer the question.

ILLUSTRATION:
"Tell me about the worst boss you've ever had."

> **Answer X** (low road):
> "The worst boss I've ever had was the director of the department who put me in charge of a program and never gave me any direction for what was required or what she expected whatsoever. She would show up late for meetings and then take over after I'd done all of the preparation for the

meeting, after I'd already started running the meeting in her absence and after I'd previously covered important ground. She'd go over materials already discussed before her late arrival without verifying where we were in the process and would contradict what I'd already said, or that I was saying after she arrived, in front of the group which included coworkers and clients.

She had no respect for the day's schedule and would go off on tangents and take up lots of time without any consideration for the timeframes that had been set, the speakers who were on the agenda in the next portion of the meeting, or the topics that needed to be covered before we could move on to and be prepared for the next topic."

Answer Y (high road/same question/ same situation/same boss):

"The worst boss I've ever had was the director of the department who put me totally in charge of a highly visible program involving coworkers and clients. She had so much confidence in my judgment and ability to head up the program that she gave me total autonomy and control over it and trusted me completely to do everything required without any input from her at all. She actually not only gave me no input, she barely even showed up for meetings to participate in them or oversee what I was doing.

It was early in my career and when I was hired I'd been so excited about working so closely with her because she headed the department, was very well known and had so much more experience than I had in the field. I'd been looking forward to how much I would gain and learn from her and how much direction she could give me in my career. Instead, she looked to me for all of the answers and direction and my career growth had to come from what I learned in the doing rather than from what I could get from her.

It was very disappointing and at the same time very rewarding. I gained a level of experience and established a reputation of excellence for myself that I'd have never been able to gain if she'd been doing her job well and had acted as the senior person in the program that I'd wanted and expected from her."

This second version is quite a different way of describing exactly the same situation and same person! Think about what serves you well and what's to your advantage as you describe negative situations to people. Even when someone's behavior is lowly or unacceptable, it's always important to demonstrate respect and make sure you're coming from a positive place when you communicate.

 **REMINDER:**

> **You earn no respect or esteem by treating someone disrespectfully or by using disrespectful or negative ways of describing a person or situation.**

PRONG 3 – BE A STORY TELLER – LIVE EXAMPLES WORK BEST

One of the most effective ways to sound confident and to overcome nervousness or artificiality in communication is to be a story teller. When you're describing actual positive experiences you've had, your communication becomes quite natural and energized because you're re-experiencing what happened and you're seeing yourself in a positive situation. When you're describing an actual experience that occurred and you're using it as an illustration for the point you want to make, you will sound much more believable than when you use a hypothetical or theoretical description or try to use facts or data to convince people of your genuineness or authenticity.

ILLUSTRATIVE SCENARIO:

Mark K. works for a publishing company and is being considered for an internal promotion in another division of the company. In the first meeting to explore if this transition will work, his potential new manager says to him, "This position interfaces with some extremely senior people with huge egos. We have a lot of prima donnas in this Division and a lot of people with very sensitive temperaments. We're looking for someone to fill this role who's exceptionally diplomatic and is known for a calm and patient demeanor with difficult demanding people."

Compare two replies that Mark might say:

✗ "I think it's very important to be respectful of all people and I'd be quite careful and attentive in how I'd interact with everyone. I'm totally comfortable and confident with difficult demanding high level executives."

✓ "I'm known for being a diplomat. Whenever I pass our CEO in the hallway, he always says, 'Good morning, Mr. Ambassador' because he's seen how well and diplomatically I've handled some extraordinarily difficult people and he appreciates how smoothly and easily I meet the challenges they present. He's said to me many times that he's always amazed that I stay so calm in the face of people's extreme behavior."

Certainly both of these responses speak to the fact that Mark is comfortable and confident in situations where he's interacting with difficult senior individuals. The main difference between the two is the second response is a "live" example that *demonstrates* these qualities unlike the first which simply lays a claim to these characteristics and does nothing to support that assertion. Of course, when you use live examples, they must be true and representative of the actual topic at hand. Also note the advantage you gain when you can use a direct quote to support what you want to convey.

PRONG 4 – TOSS THOSE QUALIFIERS

In Chapter 4, the second tool in the *Speak Easy Toolbox* warned against the repeated and habitual use of qualifying and limiting vocabulary and phrases like these:

> ***some, a little, probably, maybe,***
> ***might be, trying to,***
> ***kind of, sort of, only just, I guess***

If you use these limiters and qualifiers regularly, you will greatly dilute and take away from your professional presence and communication effectiveness. While the use of any of them occasionally here and there is harmless, when they're used in abundance, an erosion of communication occurs which can reflect a basic struggle with self-confidence. These are the kinds of words and phrases that can become so embedded over time that it can be a major challenge to eliminate them.

As long as you see and describe your experience as limited, you will convey self-doubt and will certainly not be seen as having professional presence or as being a thought leader.

AVOID: "I've **only just** done that **once** before."
BETTER: **"I have experience doing that."**

AVOID: "I **guess** we could **probably** do that."
BETTER: **"Here's how we could do that."**

AVOID: "I have **some** marketing experience and have done **a little** of that."
BETTER: **"Yes, I have marketing experience and have done direct mail campaigns."**

AVOID: "**Maybe**, this idea **might** work"
BETTER: **"I see this as a viable option and want to recommend this path."**

AVOID: "What we're **trying** to do is xxx."
BETTER: **"Our goal is to xxx." or "We have set xxx as our objective." or "What we want very much to accomplish is xxx."**

REMINDER:

> *When you say you're <u>trying</u> to do a task, you're indicating <u>zero accomplishment.</u> When you say you've set a goal to accomplish something, you've already accomplished setting the goal and you're in the process of reaching your objective.*

Limitations place the emphasis on what's missing rather than on what exists. Habitually qualifying chips away at the substance of what you have to offer and who you are professionally. Exaggeration and false bravado, at the other end of the spectrum, are equally undesirable communication characteristics. You can eliminate qualifiers from your speech patterns without replacing them with exaggerations and misrepresentations. The goal is to focus on what exists without adding disclaimers, doubt, and hesitancy. Use communication that says you take ownership and pride in what you do and who you are.

PRONG 5 – AIM STRAIGHT FOR THE TARGET

When I advise people to be selectively honest in their communication, they often giggle a bit and smile knowingly, thinking I'm suggesting they fabricate responses and make claim to accomplishments that aren't their own. These concepts are the farthest possible from the ones I want to convey; my recommendations are:

Never distort! Never misrepresent!

"SELECTIVE HONESTY" means to target your communications selectively and avoid self-revealing broad-based confessions or testimonials that tell all, leaving you exposed in ways that are unnecessary and unbeneficial. If you aim your communications directly at the bull's eye instead, you can become skilled and fluent in targeting your responses to your advantage and to the listener's focus as well.

Even when your comments are innocent and harmless, when you forget to target your communications, you can unknowingly be diminishing your professionalism and potential for recognition and advancement.

ILLUSTRATIONS:

Situation 1:	Untargeted Response:	Targeted Response: (Selective Honesty)
Request to lead a seminar for a client by an account manager/colleague at work.	"I always go skiing with my son on Martin Luther King's birthday so I was wondering if you could change the date of the meeting to another day or if not, could you get someone else to lead the session?"	"I have a long-standing commitment for Monday, the 16th and would like for us to change the date of the session if that's possible so that I can still lead the seminar for your client."
Situation 2:	**Untargeted Response:**	**Targeted Response: (Selective Honesty)**
Job interviewer in a high energy, highly competitive sales environment, asking, "You've told me about you professionally; now tell me about you personally."	"I'd have to say that my personal life is kind of empty right now because I'm in the middle of a divorce and not feeling on solid ground. I'd feel more comfortable talking about me professionally, to tell you the truth."	"One of the first things that comes to mind about me personally is how athletic I am. I jump rope 2,000 times a day and play tennis several days a week."

Situation 3:	Untargeted Response:	Targeted Response: (Selective Honesty)
Manager asking: "We'd like to ask you to leave customer service to join the marketing team, but we see how many times you've changed, directions, departments, and jobs, or been out there on your own entrepreneurially. We need to think about how this would work. Why should we select you for this new role in marketing?"	"I know how many times I've changed directions and I have been out there on my own a couple of times too. I don't want to keep changing like that anymore and I definitely don't want to be out there on my own again. If you give me this chance in the marketing department, I'm going to stick around and make this work this time for sure. I don't really want to keep changing my focus all the time anymore."	"That's an excellent question and I'm glad that you asked it. I've carefully managed my career so that I would gain exposure to a wide variety of settings in preparation for a role in marketing. Because of all the arenas I've been in, I bring a wide knowledge base and highly valuable relationships that will give me a huge advantage on our marketing team. As entrepreneurial as I am, I've learned that I bring much more value working collaboratively on a team, with the kind of research and administrative resources we have here at XYZ than I ever brought to my own independent businesses. I'm quite clear that this is the role I want now and have been preparing for over the last ten years."

There's a natural down-to-earth quality that needs to accompany this focus on targeting your communications. If the way you speak becomes inauthentic, packaged or plastic, you will miss not only the bull's eye, you will miss the target altogether. Seeking a communication coach or getting feedback from trusted peers will be an important component of developing new targeted ways of communicating.

PRONG 6 – YOU KNOW WHAT THEY SAY ABOUT ASSUMPTIONS
We've always heard what happens when you assume:

= u

= me

If we look again at our previous example of the individual with the multiple work experiences who answered the question about having such a checkered background in Situation 3, we will find, in addition to the components of the **Untargeted** versus the **Targeted**, selectively honest response, there are quite different operating assumptions underlying the two contrasting responses: In the first answer, the assumptions are negative and self-defeating and in the second answer, the underlying premises are self-confident and self-promoting. Let's examine them again:

Situation 3: (repeated)	Untargeted Response:	Targeted Response: (Selective Honesty)
Manager asking: "We'd like to ask you to leave customer service to join the marketing team, but we see how many times you've changed, directions, departments, and jobs, or been out there on your own ... **ETC.**	"I know how many times I've changed directions and I have been out there on my own a couple of times too. I don't want to keep changing like that anymore and I definitely don't want to be out there on my own again. **ETC.**	"That's an excellent question and I'm glad you asked it. I have carefully managed my career so I would gain exposure to a wide variety of settings in preparation for a role in marketing. Because of all the arenas I've been in, I bring a wide knowledge ... **ETC.**
Situation 3:	**Negative Assumptions:**	**Affirmative Premises:**
	"They don't want to promote me to the marketing team."	"They want me to demonstrate how my experience fits the promotion to the marketing department."
	"They think I won't stay in any job for very long."	"They want me to show them that I'm ready to stay in this position."
	"They think that eventually I'll want to be in business for myself again."	"They want to see how my entrepreneurial experience is the right background to make this commitment."

Situation 2 also provides a good look into how negative assumptions can take you down the wrong path and how affirmative premises can pave the way to avoid communication danger:

Situation 2: (repeated)	Untargeted Response:	Targeted Response: (Selective Honesty)
Job interviewer in a high energy, highly competitive sales environment, asking, "You've told me about you professionally; now tell me about you personally."	"I'd have to say that my personal life is kind of empty right now because I am in the middle of a divorce and not feeling on solid ground. I'd feel more comfortable talking about me professionally, to tell you the truth."	"One of the first things that comes to mind about me personally is how athletic I am. I jump rope 2,000 times a day and play tennis several days a week."
Situation 2: (repeated)	Negative Assumptions:	Affirmative Premises:
	"My personal life is terrible right now and I'm going to have to talk about that." "I don't have anything personal to say that's any of their business."	"I can select something to say that is unrelated to how terrible my personal life is." "They're a very high energy and competitive group so I can use my athleticism to answer the question."
	"That's an inappropriate question to ask me on a job interview."	"Rather than focus on how much I dislike this question, I can stay focused on presenting what I want them to know about me rather than reveal something personal that's none of their business and irrelevant."

Negative assumptions provide the foundation for defensive and self-defeating communication. When you begin with an affirmative premise, your communication will naturally shift to reflect a positive and confident perspective.

PRONG 7 - INCONSISTENCY ALWAYS BITES YOU ON YOUR BACKSIDE

If you say that you have great crisis management skills at work in one breath and you're impatient with family members in the next, there's a contradiction and inconsistency that you're demonstrating in your communications. Even if the inconsistency – impatience – relates to children at home in a non-business environment, it rings a false note that someone who claims a strength in crisis management would choose a self-description like impatience. This type of inconsistency will be particularly striking during a job interview when people are learning about someone unknown to them. On an every day basis at work, there will also be an underlying awareness of inconsistencies. If you want to be seen as a professional and you want to advance in your career, it's important to be aware of how these subtle inconsistencies in your communications can influence how you're seen and how your opportunities for advancement can be measured against them.

COMPARE TWO COMMENTS FROM THE SAME PERSON FOR CONSISTENCY:

1. *"I'm very good in a crisis environment. There have been times when our Director was ready to call in Security because our customers were so irate that violence was ready to erupt. I have such a calming effect on people that when I walk into the room and begin quietly talking to people one at a time, they get calm right away and Security is no longer needed."*

2. *"The hardest part of being a single mom is that I'm really impatient with my two-year-old daughter but I guess all moms are like that."*

COMPARE TWO COMMENTS FROM THE SAME PERSON FOR CONSISTENCY:

1. *"I want to be in charge of all communications, scheduling, and oversight for our national training programs across the entire company."*

2. *"I know myself and my style very well and I'm just not a detail oriented person."*

The concept is to pay attention to what you're conveying to people. We all have competing characteristics and circumstances in our lives. Life is full of paradox. The point is to be aware of what you are communicating before blurting out whatever comes into your head. Spontaneity is lovely and communication that is artificial and packaged is quite unappealing. It still makes sense to think about the main points you want to convey to others and make sure that whatever topic you're talking about reflects consistency and definitely avoids contradiction. In so many cases, when the subject matter is diverse, we often forget about the connections that lie between various topics.

Career fitness is vital for success and satisfaction. Once again let's look at the career communication exercise regimen as a package and make the career workout part of every workday. The payoff will be that over time all of these behaviors and communications will become so second nature that they will be completely natural and effortless.

YOUR CAREER GYM COMMUNICATION WORKOUT

1. Be prepared.
2. Be positive.
3. Give "live" illustrations.
4. Avoid limiting qualifiers.
5. Be focused.
6. Avoid negative assumptions.
7. Be consistent.

Speak Easy Rules

Review and Summary:

10 | Working It At Work

✓ Recognize how important positive communication is.

✓ Give 100% to being well-prepared.

✓ Speak with focus and direction.

✓ Base your communication on affirmative premises.

✓ Describe your strengths and actions in consistent terms.

11 | Getting What You Want

In traveling across our communications landscape, negotiation is a topic that each of us will encounter in some way. In a prior chapter, the term NETWORKING was replaced with R&R (Research and Relationships) for emphasis, for repositioning and for clarification of definition. In this chapter, the term NEGOTIATE will be interchanged with REACH AGREEMENT, also for emphasis and repositioning, and primarily to take the focus away from the competition to achieve gain and to avoid loss. Negotiation conveys the image of the boxing match and conjures up the impression of a contest with its accompanying tally of gains and losses, or more strikingly, of winners and losers.

Terms Of Agreement

The more you can see NEGOTIATING as the quest to REACH AGREEMENT, the more effective your negotiating communications will be. And the less you use the word NEGOTIATE when you're negotiating with someone, the easier it will be to reach your negotiation objectives. The word NEGOTIATE intimidates and threatens; it puts people on guard; it's like a call to battle; it often feels exactly like conflict.

Getting what you want at any cost is too big a price to pay. A do-or-die approach to negotiation opens the door for ultimatum, a card you would only want to play in the rarest of circumstances. There's no wiggle room or further negotiation once an ultimatum has been given. If you're at the point of giving someone an ultimatum, make sure you're ready to walk away empty-handed or to deliver the threatened punishment. At the other end of the spectrum, making it your goal to find ways to reach agreement creates a playing field with endless room to navigate and limitless options to offer and choose from.

WIN-WIN WINS AGAIN

Here's a list incorporating the style of language variations that will increase the likelihood of getting the most in a negotiation. Using these types of communications will also enhance how the other person in the negotiation sees what he or she's gaining and giving up. And lastly, these approaches will go a long way to keep interactions from escalating into conflict.

- ✓ "**Let's keep talking** so that we can **get this right for both** of us."
- ✓ "Here are the topics we need to find ways to **reach agreement** about."
- ✓ "I'm committed to finding the right way to **make this happen**."
- ✓ "I know we can determine how to **reach our goals** in a way that **will be good for both of us**."
- ✓ "I'm **confident we can agree on … .**"
- ✓ "Let's examine ways to do XXX so we can **finalize our agreement**."
- ✓ "Let's look at how to **make this equitable for everyone involved**."

OPPOSITES COMPETE

It's human nature to see circumstances from a one-sided and personal perspective. To reach agreement in a conflict or in a negotiation requires looking beyond self-interest and finding a balance that incorporates collaboration, compromise and inclusion. This requires focusing on your own goals without doing so at the expense of others, without sacrificing someone else's well-being for your own advancement.

If reaching agreement is the true objective instead of creating a winner and loser, the likelihood of using effective communication and completing a successful negotiation in a timely manner increases dramatically.

ABOUT THOSE NUMBERS: THE MONEY GAME

When it comes to negotiating your annual salary increase or your new job compensation package, there are some hard and fast communication rules that can increase a good outcome.

- Whoever names numbers first is in a weaker position. Get the other person to talk about numbers first.

- Whenever possible, postpone the discussion of numbers until after an offer has been made.

- Do your homework and know what the salaries and compensation ranges are REALISTICALLY in your field and in your geography.

- Name ranges rather than a specific number if you're compelled to state compensation numbers.

- Without greed as the goal, ask what the employer's flexibility is.

Here are communications that match these guidelines:

- ✓ "Let's talk about salary later. I'm so interested in hearing more about this position. I know we'll be able to agree on numbers when we're at the point where we both agree this is exactly the right position for me."

- ✓ "What's the range for this position? I'd be very interested in hearing more about that."

- ✓ "When I began this job search, I promised myself I'd keep my salary history and all compensation numbers out of the conversations I'd have with people. I want to make sure my decision and my future employer's decision about a job offer is based on how right the fit is and how much value I'll bring to the company. I know we'll be able to agree on the numbers if everything else is right."

- ✓ "I began my career at XYZ when I was eighteen years old, just out of high school. I put myself through college at night and have continued to work for XYZ until now. My salary there today is based on my starting salary as a high school graduate, in spite of the fact that all of my clients are Fortune 500 corporations and all of the accounts I manage are multi-million-dollar accounts. Based on my research and success, I know my value in the job market today is in the mid six figure range."

- ✓ "I did extensive research and spoke to people I respect highly to get your name. The reason I'm speaking to you today is because of your outstanding reputation as an executive recruiter. I *know you've been placing key people in my industry and are an expert on what the right compensation range would be for a professional with the background and experience that I have. Since I've worked for XYZ since I was eighteen years old, my salary there today is based on my starting salary as a high school graduate. What do you see as the range for someone with my background and expertise who manages Fortune 500 multi-million dollar accounts? I know because of how successful you are that you have your finger right on the pulse of the marketplace and really know what the right range is for someone like me."*

✓ *"I'm so pleased with this offer. I've thought about all that we discussed very carefully and see how good a fit this is and how well I'll be able to do xxxxxxx, yyyyyyy, and zzzzzzz. I am particularly pleased about qqqqqqq. There are some topics I'd like to talk more to you about. Please describe further blah, etc. and blah. What is your flexibility on the compensation for this position? I am especially interested in hearing how you see the components we just discussed as they relate to the compensation. Let's keep talking about all of this so we can make this right for both of us and finalize our agreement."*

BALANCE ISN'T ALWAYS EQUAL

Reaching an equitable or satisfactory agreement usually has pluses and minuses for both sides. Since self-interest is a primary human objective, the views and goals on either side of a negotiation are unlikely to be identical. Rather than look for a 50/50 exactly-equal deal, it's better to define what's desirable and equitable in terms of priorities, weighting of

importance and long-term objectives. Going into a negotiation with as much definition and clarity as possible will
provide perspective and objectivity which are challenging
to maintain in a demanding negotiation or conflict resolution situation. Here's a grid that can help you prepare for a
negotiation. (It's also useful for decision-making in analyz-
ing various options you are considering.):

PREPARATION FOR NEGOTIATION

INSTRUCTIONS:

1. Start by writing out as many separate negotiation
objectives as you can. Even if some of them are
not on the negotiating table, include everything
that you can define in your ideal outcome.

2. In the designated boxes, write the measurable
gains and losses and the components of approval
and disapproval for each objective.

3. When you've fleshed out all of the objectives and
the elements that go with each of them, prioritize
the objectives as to their value to you and place
a number designating their importance to you on
the grid. (See sample.)

4. Place an **X** next to any objective that is a deal
breaker for you, that will cause you to withdraw
from the negotiation if you can't obtain it. Make it
a goal to have no Xs on your grid if possible.

SAMPLE PREPARATION FOR SALARY AND JOB OFFER NEGOTIATION

(These are hypothetical points that an individual may have. Notice that some contradict each other or could be seen in an opposite category by another person.)

Negotiation Objectives	Measurable Gains	Measurable Losses	Approval Self/Others (Intangible gains)	Disapproval Self/Others (Intangible losses)
Objective A #4 Director Title	>Executive business card >Management committee member	>Loss of non exempt status >Longer work hours/no overtime pay	>Status >Respect	>More time away from family
Objective B #3 Relocation Reimbursement	>Moving expenses paid >Access to museums, theater	>Leaving old house restored by hand, blood sweat & tears	>Arts/culture environment >Classier life	>Losing community >Little fish, big pond feeling
Objective C #8 Corner Office/ View	>Next door to President >In executive suite	>Bull pen environment and brainstorming component lost	>Breathing room >Stress reduction	>Isolated from action >May be seen as aloof
Objective D #5 20% Salary Increase	>More goodies >Credit card paid off	>More money = more temptation to spend	>"Made-it" feeling	>Old friends feeling intimidated
Objective E #2 Reporting to President	>More decision making authority >More exposure at senior level	>Too visible >Warts/mistakes on view all the time	>Connected at high levels	>Seen as snob or aloof
Objective F #6 Executive Coach/360 Feedback	>Professional development >Feedback	>Extra work required >Double time to get job done	>Seen as high potential	>Some may think coach is for problem behaviors
Objective G #1 Tuition Reimbursement	>MBA credential >More earning power >Savings on cost of education	>No tax advantage	>Go getter >Self- motivated	>People think I'm never satisfied with what I already have
Objective H #7 Company Car	>No car/ insurance payments >Not driving old unsafe car	>Can't park new car on street >Garage payments	>Safety of newer model car >No one questioning about my jalopy	>Another object that could cause jealousy of friends/family

PREPARATION FOR NEGOTIATION

Negotiation Objectives	Measurable Gains	Measurable Losses	Approval Self/Others (Intangible gains)	Disapproval Self/Others (Intangible losses)
Objective A				
Objective B				
Objective C				
Objective D				
Objective E				
Objective F				
Objective G				
Objective H				

Defining your objectives and creating a carefully thought out wish list with all of the obvious and underlying pros and cons is highly beneficial. It will give you clarity and objectivity as a strong foundation for negotiating. It's imperative that you refrain from thinking of this preparation as a *greed list*. Your success in negotiating will come from reaching an equitable agreement rather than from getting every item on your list.

LET'S KEEP TALKING

A highly valuable precept in negotiating communications is that of continuing the dialogue in order to reach an agreement. If you express a desire and demonstrate the staying power to keep talking constructively, you will be able to influence the outcome of the conversation in a proactive and meaningful way. It's critical to be aware of the distinction between expressing, "Let's keep talking" and simply *digging in*. The lyrics of the old Kenny Rogers poker song, *The Gambler*, are quite apropos:

> **"You've got to know when to hold 'em,
> know when to fold 'em
> Know when to walk away,
> know when to run."**

Good communication skills can keep the exchange from becoming a debate, an argument, a conflict or a stalemate. There are so many excellent ways to communicate that can come into play to keep the flow of negotiation on track and moving in a forward direction toward a mutually agreeable conclusion.

Speak Easy Rules

Review and Summary:

11 | Getting What You Want

✓ Think of negotiating as reaching agreement.

✓ Offer various options to get the results you want.

✓ Target what you say to your advantage.

✓ Define your objectives before engaging in negotiations.

✓ Recognize the value of patience and staying power.

12 | Facing An Audience

There's one remaining visit to make on our communication journey together. Most of us will make a public presentation at some point. Countless individuals are quite uncomfortable speaking in front of any size group. Often people's career advancement is tied to their ability to make presentations to small groups, larger meetings or even conferences.

PRESENTING WITH EASE AND IMPACT
To face an audience with authority, confidence and ease is an ultimate communication skill. Let's see if we can take some of the mystery and intimidation out of public speaking so that no matter how frightening or uncomfortable it feels to you, you will be able to find new approaches and perspectives that will always be there for you to reduce anxiety and contribute to confidence and comfort.

ADRENALINE GETS YOU GOING – THE GOOD OLD FEAR FACTOR
Many of the world's most accomplished presenters and performers suffer horribly from stage fright. It's rare for a person to present to an audience without some form of nervousness or stress. When you realize the beneficial component of adrenaline, you can begin to be more accepting of the physical feelings that accompany fear.

One extremely accomplished and well known British actor revealed that he gets so nervous before going on stage that he vomits into a paper bag before every performance. As much distress as he has, he also says that he knows that without this level of discomfort, he would not be able to give a good performance. He knows something is wrong and his acting will be poor, if he doesn't have the level of stage fright that produces nausea. As extreme as this practice and belief is, it illustrates the positive value of adrenaline and stage fright.

If we examine the origin of the human adrenal gland function, we will recognize that the initial evolutionary purpose of the rush of adrenaline was to provide super physical responses to life-threatening attack. If danger was lurking, the flow of adrenaline would produce raised hair on the back of the neck, goose bumps on the skin, chills down the spine, extremely rapid heart rate, outpouring of perspiration, and intensity in breathing, all combining to increase awareness and enhance physical prowess such as running faster or increased muscle strength. We experience fear today through these same physical adrenal characteristics which remain quite similar, when we sense danger and feel fear, even when there's zero physical danger involved. When we stop and consider what it feels like to be extremely excited about an upcoming event that we're looking forward to with great pleasure, we can recognize that the physical characteristics of fear are quite similar to wonderful anticipatory excitement: goose bumps on the skin, chills down the spine, extremely rapid heart rate, outpouring of perspiration, intensity in breathing. Since there's this striking similarity in what excitement and fear feel like, we can convince ourselves to be more daring, by exchanging our views so we can begin to enjoy the stimulation and motivation that fear provides.

Clearly there are no life-threatening dangers associated with public speaking, yet people often have such immobilizing fear related to it that their sense of physical well-being feels severely threatened. It's quite helpful to examine your belief system about what will happen when you present to an audience or speak to a small group of people. Here are some of the responses people say when asked what their fears are relating to speaking publicly:

- *"I'll die of embarrassment."*
- *"I'll completely forget what I'm saying and draw a total blank."*
- *"I won't be able to breathe."*
- *"I just can't do it. I feel like I'll be paralyzed."*
- *"I won't be able to speak because I'm so terrified."*
- *"I'll make a fool of myself."*
- *"I'll be so nervous that people will start laughing."*
- *"No one will have a clue what I'm talking about."*
- *"I just hate exposing myself that way. I always feel so naked."*
- *"I know how boring I'll be. I don't want people to see me that way."*

Most of these exaggerated fears can be greatly reduced if not completely eliminated through these approaches:

✓ 1. **Examine the validity of the fears, redefining them with less volatile and more realistic language and connecting them with doable goals to offset the fears.**
✓ 2. **Create safety nets and protective devices to counter balance the components of the fears.**
✓ 3. **Embrace new operating platforms that will enhance perspectives and diminish fears.**
✓ 4. **Gain presentation comfort through practice in safe rehearsal venues, acquiring extended presentation mileage over time.**

Let's examine each of these four approaches one at a time and identify solid and satisfying ways to counter-balance the fears we have about speaking in front of a group:

✓ **1. Examine the validity of the fears, redefining them with less volatile and more realistic language and connecting them with doable goals to offset the fears:**

EXTREME FEAR: *"I'll die of embarrassment."*
REALITY: *"I'm afraid I'll embarrass myself by doing a poor job."*
GOAL: *"I'll need to prepare well to avoid embarrassing myself."*

EXTREME FEAR: *"I won't be able to breathe."*
REALITY: *"When I feel very nervous I sometimes forget to breathe and I even hold my breath."*
GOAL: *"I'll make sure I focus on breathing deeply and slowly prior to my presentation and will use relaxation breathing techniques to help me relax and breathe calmly."*

✓ **2. Create safety nets and protective devices to counter balance the components of the fears:**

EXTREME FEAR: *"I won't be able to speak at all because I'm so terrified."*

REALITY: *"When I get up to speak in front of an audience my throat gets very dry and my voice sounds very weak."*

DEVICE: *"I'll have water at the podium and a microphone to make sure my voice is clear for my presentation."*

EXTREME FEAR: *"I'll completely forget what I'm saying and just draw a total blank."*

REALITY: *"When I'm nervous, it is difficult to think clearly and remember what I want to say."*

DEVICE: *"I'll type and print out my entire presentation in large print, on both sides of the page, double spaced, with highlighted key words and phrases. I'll put my presentation in a three ring binder so it's easy to keep the pages in front of me as I present. I'll carefully code the pages with the slides I'm using. There'll be no moment in my presentation when I can't find my place and the words I want to say."*

✓3. Embrace new operating platforms that will enhance perspectives and diminish fears:

EXTREME FEAR: *"No one will have a clue what I'm trying to convey."*

REALITY: *"It's important to me that people understand what I'm talking about."*

TACTICS: *"I'll ask strong open-ended pre-prepared questions to the audience during my presentation to engage people and to be sure they understand the material well. I'll* *encourage discussion and answer questions from the audience as well."*

EXTREME FEAR: *"I'll make a fool of myself."*
REALITY: *"I want to sound like I know what I'm talking about."*
TACTICS: *"I'll conduct a survey prior to my presentation and find out what people most want to know about my topic. I'll include my survey findings in my presentation and will speak to people informally prior to my presentation to test and to ensure my points are easily understandable."*

✓ 4. Gain presentation comfort through practice in safe rehearsal venues and through extended presentation mileage over time.

EXTREME FEAR: *"I just hate exposing myself in front of an audience. I always feel so naked."*
REALITY: *"It will take a while before I can begin to feel comfortable making a presentation."*
PRACTICE: *"I'll invite some close friends to my home to practice my presentation. I'll ask them to critique me and give me suggestions about improvements I can make."*

EXTREME FEAR: *"I know how boring I'll be. I don't want people to see me that way."*
REALITY: *"I want to have a dynamic presence and be engaged with my audience."*
PRACTICE: *"I'll tape my presentation and critique it myself. I'll also ask a professional coach to partner with me to enhance my presenta-*

tion fluidity and professionalism. I'll take my show on the road to a few smaller groups and organizations so when the annual conference takes place, I'll be smooth and ready."

REMINDERS:

> → **Stage fright can be a significant contributor to enhancing performance.**
> → **Characteristics of fear are similar to wonderful anticipatory excitement.**
> → **Our personal belief system about public speaking can sabotage us.**

HEY, IT'S JUST TALKING – YOU CAN DO THAT

There is usually a huge contrast between how easily a person speaks informally on an ad hoc basis to one or two people, or even in an informal group of people, and how nervous and uncomfortable that same person becomes while making a presentation on the exact same topic to a larger audience in a formal capacity. ***The trick is to be able to think of public speaking in the same way you think of talking about a topic you know a lot about, in an everyday conversation.*** If you picture in your mind's eye those people you can easily talk to and then address individuals in your audience as if they are those people, ***imagining that you're having a conversation rather than making a presentation***, it will add greatly to your sounding natural and comfortable while presenting.

There are differing views on whether presentations should

be memorized verbatim, read word for word, spoken freely from a detailed outline or presented extemporaneously. Actually all of these styles can be quite effective, if done well. It really depends on the preferences of the individual presenter and on the occasion for the presentation. One person might be very comfortable presenting a eulogy without a prewritten text. Another person might want to have every spoken word carved in stone for such a juncture.

Since so many approaches can be successful, it's important to identify the underlying ingredients that can contribute to the success of these varying styles. When a speaker demonstrates the following starred characteristics, the delivery method becomes unimportant:

ESSENTIAL PUBLIC SPEAKING CHARACTERISTICS

★*NATURAL AND CONVERSATIONAL*

★*ENTHUSIASTIC AND PASSIONATE*

★*DOWN-TO-EARTH AND HUMAN*

★*RESPONSIVE AND ENGAGING*

★*ENERGIZING AND UPLIFTING*

Think of the many teachers you've had over your lifetime. What made some of them great, some of them mediocre and some of them horrendous? It wasn't really about how much they knew; it was about how much passion they brought to the classroom. It wasn't so much about how smart they were; it was much more about how much they challenged you to think, how much they engaged your mind, how much they connected with their students. It wasn't actually about what they said; it was about how they said it.

STICK WITH WHAT YOU KNOW BEST

The most important starting place for any kind of public speaking or presentation is to make sure the presentation topic is one you are completely comfortable with and thoroughly knowledgeable about. If you're asked to present a topic you're unfamiliar with, request to change the topic to another subject that you know well, learn about the requested unknown topic to the point of intimacy, or else decline to make the presentation. As a presenter, when you feel that you're in your element and you "own" the subject matter, you will have the greatest potential for conveying the starred essential public speaking characteristics featured above.

JUST FOR FUN

Before you even begin to plan out a presentation, deciding what to include or when to say what, make a list of all of the facts you know about your selected topic that you find fascinating, provocative and interesting, without thinking of your presentation or your audience at all. If you're not actually making a presentation on a topic, and want to go through this exercise, you can pick any topic you know well and are passionate about.

When this first list has all of the facets you find most appealing, make a second list of all of the most fascinating questions you can think of about your topic. Include those you know the answers to and those you're most curious about knowing the answers to.

When this second list is complete, make a third list of all the ingredients you see as critically important for other people to know about your topic or you think will have an impact in the world in some small or significant way.

LIST 1: MOST INTERESTING ASPECTS
LIST 2: MOST FASCINATING QUESTIONS
LIST 3: MOST IMPORTANT / HIGHEST IMPACT FACTS

There can be overlap on the three lists and the language and descriptions can be free flowing and personal. These lists are stream-of-consciousness lists and, for the moment, for your eyes only. Make sure you're creating these lists for your pleasure and amusement and while making them, remain disconnected from the fact that you will be making a presentation on this topic.

When you feel you have exhausted the limits of all three lists, review the combined lists thoughtfully to select what you consider to be your topic's **Top Ten** components based on these following three important characteristics:

CHARACTERISTICS FOR TOP TEN SELECTIONS
1. You are most passionately connected to them
2. You are very comfortable talking about them
3. You think these are the most significant elements

Select your **Top Ten** factors only. Do not limit this list to less than ten nor increase the number to more than ten.

If there's a natural combination of more than one point from your three lists that truly collapses into a single entity, you can merge ingredients to end up with your **Top Ten** list. Remember that the goal is to have fun. You're still in a pre-

presentation thinking mode. This is more about your personal guideposts of interest and connection to the topic.

Examine your **Top Ten** list to see if you are completely satisfied that all ten points meet the above three requirements and totally merit a **Top Ten** designation.

At this point, there's one more task to do before you return to the major undertaking of creating your actual presentation. When you're satisfied with your **Top Ten** list, choose three people you will share its contents with separately and individually. There are two requirements for this:

> **REQUIREMENT 1:**
> Describe the contents of your Top Ten list <u>face-to-face</u>, rather than on the phone, via email, text message, or in writing.

> **REQUIREMENT 2:**
> Share all ten components from the Top Ten list with each of the three individuals <u>without</u> including the additional remaining contents from your primary three lists.

You can use any platform you want for this in-person conversation. You can say it's an exercise from a book you're reading, a way for you to get comfortable talking about the topic to prepare for your presentation, and/or that you're passionate about the topic and simply want to discuss it.

Making the three lists, selecting the most critical factors from them, limiting what you select, and sharing the **Top Ten** list with others are wonderful ways to set the stage for you to tackle public speaking. You can use this exercise to move towards overcoming your anxieties; you can use it to become more aware of the important basic ingredients that go into making a presentation resonate for both speaker and listener; you can use the methodology as the foundation for an actual presentation.

SEE YOURSELF DOING IT – GETTING BEYOND STIFF

The second critical factor to achieve the **ESSENTIAL PUBLIC SPEAKING CHARACTERISTICS** will be to fill your presentations with actual stories or experiences that demonstrate and enliven the concepts and information you are presenting. There's a deadly stiffness in presentations when speakers come across as removed from their subject matter. When a presenter shares real stories, vivid illustrations or live examples, that stiffness will dissipate and these desired features will blossom. The **ESSENTIAL PUBLIC SPEAKING CHARACTERISTICS** will naturally emerge and will fluidly become wonderful factors for getting beyond stiff, so that you will come across as:

> ★ *NATURAL AND CONVERSATIONAL*
>
> ★ *ENTHUSIASTIC AND PASSIONATE*
>
> ★ *DOWN-TO-EARTH AND HUMAN*
>
> ★ *RESPONSIVE AND ENGAGING*
>
> ★ *ENERGIZING AND UPLIFTING*

See yourself in action, tell those related stories that represent the topics best, and share conversations with actual quotes that demonstrate your points, and you will find yourself exhibiting these key qualities and feeling at ease standing in front of an audience like never before.

Excitement Is Contagious

If you have genuine enthusiasm for your topic and allow yourself to share that excitement publicly, there will be a wonderful spillover effect for your audience. There are many ways to demonstrate fervor without sacrificing what feels instinctive to you or changing your natural style and preferences. The more you can find comfortable ways to demonstrate your passion for your subject, the more involved your audience will become and the easier it will be for you to be a public speaker.

Speak Easy Rules

Review and Summary:

12 | Facing An Audience

✓ Challenge your belief system about public speaking.

✓ Realize how easy it is to talk about what you know well.

✓ See that stage fright enhances performance.

✓ Use true stories to illustrate your presentation points.

✓ Recognize how enthusiasm engages an audience.

13 | Summing It All Up – Communication, Key To The Good Life

Communication plays a critical role in every facet of human existence. The more we can enhance how we communicate, the more benefit we will receive. What becomes apparent from examining the many aspects of communication is that when we improve our communication skills, we also gain a deeper self-awareness, a richer emotional maturity, and a more informed psychological strength.

On a larger scale, if each of us makes effective communication a primary objective, it will bring great value to our families, our friends, our homes, our workplaces, our communities, our nations, and our world.

THE VERY FIRST TOOL

With the dawn of human existence came the first forms of communication. Before there were actual words, before there was true language, before fire was tamed and weapons were created, before tools were crafted, before all that separates humans from other species on earth, there was primitive communication.

The first communications were facial grimaces, and grunts of pain or pleasure. There were gestures of hostility and caresses of affection. There was first laughter and there were first tears. Sexual expression and reproduction also contributed to the birth of communication. In a sense, communication was the very first human tool.

Those first human communication sounds and expressions spawned thousands of different languages. There are **more than 6,500 known languages** spoken in the world. These languages have varying vocabulary, sentence formation, alphabets and written symbols.

With all of these language variations, the basic forms of communication remain universal. Facial expressions for pain, anger, surprise, fear, joy, confusion, and sorrow are communicated in the same way by all human beings on our planet today no matter which language they speak, which geography they inhabit or how advanced their culture and civilization.

LIFE WITHOUT CONNECTION
Without communication there would be no bonds uniting person to person. From the smallest human scale to the grandest, communication is the means of human connection. It's inconceivable to imagine a world without communication. Art, literature, theater, science, history, sports, politics and entertainment all share the common foundation of communication.

Communication is actually as essential as air to breathe, water to drink, food to eat, shelter and clothing to protect. Take away communication and what remains?

RESPONSIBILITY ALWAYS RESIDES IN YOU
It is through communication that we can each take responsibility for what is important to us and how we exhibit that importance. If your communications are hostile, aggressive, deprecating or judgmental, your causes will be diminished and your goals will be thwarted. If you eliminate these negative qualities from your heart, from your head, and from your communications, your beliefs will be better heard and

recognized. If you take responsibility for your words and how you convey them, you will enrich your own life and the lives of those around you.

Communication is the responsibility we all share, the one common denominator each person can use to make a difference in the world.

WHEN ALL IS SAID AND DONE

It takes a lot of work to be a good communicator. Making determined and dedicated communication enhancements requires time and energy. If you can focus on the benefits of your efforts rather than on how difficult and demanding the work is, then one day, perhaps much sooner than you imagine, you will find that you've arrived and, just like second nature, you will be able to **SPEAK EASY**.

Communication is as primitive and simple as saying hello to a passerby on the street and as sophisticated and complex as describing Einstein's Theory of Relativity. It's the conduit for all truth and all lies, for all good and all evil. It's our most basic tool and our greatest challenge.

Thank you for traveling with me. Our communication journey has covered much terrain. Even though we've voyaged far and wide, we've not reached a destination. The road to enhanced communication is non-ending. Happy travels.

Speak Easy Rules

Review and Summary:

13 | Summing It All Up – Communication, Key To The Good Life

✓ Know that excellence in communication enriches life.

✓ Value what it takes to change communication patterns.

✓ See how universal basic human communication is.

✓ Take responsibility for what you say and how you say it.

✓ Be patient and determined with your communication goals.

Speak Easy Rules – Chapter Summaries

1 | Keep It Level
✓Experience a level playing field of communication.
✓Be aware of how facial expressions say more than words.
✓Monitor your voice tone to diminish dual messages.
✓Express your reactions directly without apology.
✓Focus on demonstrating respect in every communication.

2 | Tell Them That You Really Heard
✓Acknowledge what others are saying.
✓Validate others' positions before promoting your own.
✓Concentrate on listening without jumping to your views.
✓Realize you can validate others without agreeing with them.
✓Separate high standards from disapproval and judgment.

3 | There's A Good Way To Say Everything
✓Select direct ways to communicate.
✓Realize that people appreciate hearing the truth.
✓Recognize that there is no need to embellish or distort.
✓Resolve to be comfortable talking about difficult topics.
✓Use simpler descriptions and realize that less is more.

4 | Replacing Deadly Habits
✓Avoid passive or victimized language.
✓Express yourself in the affirmative.
✓Choose neutral rather than negatively-charged words.
✓Recognize the pitfalls of giving people advice.
✓Eliminate hackneyed ways of communicating.

5 | Be Your Own Best Friend
✓Get your sense of well-being from yourself.
✓Disempower abusive communicators.
✓Focus on what you have rather than on what is missing.
✓Value the gains you receive from loss.
✓Build strong systems of support.

Speak Easy Rules – Chapter Summaries

(continued)

6 | Every Style Can Be Successful

✓Appreciate what distinguishes you from other people.
✓Believe there are many good approaches to all situations.
✓Leverage your preferred style.
✓See value in expanding your communication repertoire.
✓Broaden your horizons to include wider views.

7 | Armor For Abuse

✓Dissolve people's power to hurt you with their words.
✓Recognize when silence would be the best response.
✓Thank people, without defensiveness, for being open.
✓Take care of your internal emotional trigger points.
✓Refrain from measuring yourself harshly against others.

8 | Refusing The Right Way

✓Remain at ease when people make difficult requests.
✓Validate people's right to ask for what they want.
✓Match your responses with what you can really deliver.
✓Be clear when your intention is to refuse completely.
✓Think through your response before you say yes.

9 | Expanding Your "Who You Know" Quotient

✓See NETWORKING as research and relationship building.
✓Include solutions when discussing your challenges.
✓Believe you have or can access the right contacts.
✓Share what you know when you ask important questions.
✓View NETWORKING as more than spreading your name.

Speak Easy Rules – Chapter Summaries

(continued)

10 | Working It At Work

✓Recognize how important positive communication is.
✓Give 100% to being well-prepared.
✓Speak with focus and direction.
✓Base your communication on affirmative premises.
✓Describe your strengths and actions in consistent terms.

11 | Getting What You Want

✓Think of negotiating as reaching agreement.
✓Offer various options to get the results you want.
✓Target what you say to your advantage.
✓Define your objectives before engaging in negotiations.
✓Recognize the value of patience and staying power.

12 | Facing An Audience

✓Challenge your belief system about public speaking.
✓Realize how easy it is to talk about what you know well.
✓See that stage fright enhances performance.
✓Use true stories to illustrate your presentation points.
✓Recognize how enthusiasm engages an audience.

13 | Summing It All Up –
Communication, Key To The Good Life

✓Know that excellence in communication enriches life.
✓Value what it takes to change communication patterns.
✓See how universal basic human communication is.
✓Take responsibility for what you say and how you say it.
✓Be patient and determined with your communication goals.

Speak Easy Key Word Index

Speak Easy Key Word Index

(continued)